POLITICS IN

# WEST GERMANY

## FROM SCHMIDT TO KOHL

I - J - 99

*Other titles in this Series*

Politics in Britain: From Callaghan to Thatcher
Politics in China: From Mao to Deng
Politics in France: From Giscard to Mitterrand
Politics in the Soviet Union: From Brezhnev to Gorbachev
Politics in the United States: From Carter to Reagan

**About the Series**

Chambers Political Spotlights aim to provide a bridge between
conventional textbooks and contemporary reporting. Each title
examines the key political, economic and social changes of the
country, providing, in addition, a brief contextual background to
each development discussed.

# POLITICS IN
# WEST
# GERMANY

## FROM SCHMIDT
## TO KOHL

Ian Derbyshire
Ph.D. Cantab

# Chambers

© Ian Derbyshire 1987

First published by Sandpiper Publishing as a Sandpiper Compact, 1985
This edition published by W & R Chambers Ltd, 1987
Reprinted 1988

**British Library Cataloguing in Publication Data**

Derbyshire, Ian
    Politics in West Germany: from Schmidt
to Kohl.—(Chambers political spotlights).
    1. Germany (West)—Politics and
government—1982-
    I.Title
    320.943        JN3971.A2

    ISBN 0-550-20740-6


Typeset by Outline, Edinburgh
Printed in Great Britain at the University Press, Cambridge

**Acknowledgements**

This book is based on a wide range of contemporary sources including
*The Times, The Guardian, The Independent, The Observer, The Sunday
Times, The Economist, Newsweek, Time, Keesing's Contemporary
Archives, The Annual Register* and *Europa: A World Survey.*

Every effort has been made to trace copyright holders, but if any have
inadvertently been overlooked the publishers will be pleased to make the
necessary arrangements at the first opportunity.

# Contents

# Preface

In September 1982 the defection of the FDP liberal party from the ruling coalition brought to an end thirteen years of continuous rule by the Social Democratic Party (SPD) under, first Willy Brandt and, then, Helmut Schmidt. The Christian Democratic Party (CDU) were returned to office in the March 1983 Bundestag election and looked set for another decade in power while the SPD awaited a new Machtwechsel (change of government).

This Spotlight examines the different policy programmes pursued during the late Schmidt and early Kohl eras; the growing fissures within the SPD and the concurrent emergence of the environmentalist Green Party; the splits within the FDP and between the CDU and its Bavarian sister party, the CSU; the developing conflicts over defence and economic policy; West Germany's relative performance during the 1974-76 and 1980-85 economic recessions; the southward movement in the German economy; the estrangement of the trade unions and the crumbling of the 'social market economy' consensus; the Gastarbeiter question; and foreign relations with France, the United States and East Germany. It concludes with an analysis of the January 1987 Bundestag election and its implications for the defeated left-of-centre opposition.

FIGURE 1: WEST GERMAN LÄNDER

# Part One

# WEST GERMAN POLITICAL AND CONSTITUTIONAL DEVELOPMENT

## From Empire to Weimar Republic

Political unity came late to Germany. In 1815 a large confederation of 39 principalities covered the German empire, with Prussia in the east and Habsburg Austria to the south vying for supremacy. During the 1860s Prussia, guided by its astute prime minister, Otto von Bismarck (1815 − 98), established hegemony over the smaller north German states, but not until 1871 was the polyglot German confederation fully united. A further eventful eight decades were needed before political stability and a liberal democracy was finally established.

One factor behind this laggardly democratic development had been the slow pace of industrial growth in 'late developing' Imperial Germany. There had been small pockets of industrialisation before 1850 in the Rhineland and Saxony, but it took political unification, the establishment of the free-trading *Zollverein* and the spread of railways before Germany achieved economic 'take off'. Thus at the time of the 1848 Revolution the German middle class was too weak to wrest any significant political concessions, while in the eastern half of the German empire the large semi-feudal *Junker* landlords continued to dominate. This traditional military and landed élite remained in power during the rest of the Imperial period buttressed through a nationalist and statist ideology, popularised by the romantic poets and philosophers, Goethe and Hegel, and through economic and military success. A democracy of types did emerge after 1871 with a bicameral parliament (*Reichstag*) and universal male suffrage, but it was the Prussian Emperor (*Kaiser*) and prime minister (*Chancellor*) who continued to wield real, practical power. Germany thus entered the 20th century with an autocratic and paternalistic political and economic tradition, with the state involved in numerous fields of activity — for example, sickness and old age insurance, tariff protection, and technical education.

Military defeat during the First World War finally brought the abdication of the Kaiser and the proclamation of a parliamentary republic — the Weimar Republic. This experiment with democracy was, however, short-lived, being doomed from the beginning, and it was destined to be superseded in 1933 by the autocracy of Adolf Hitler and National Socialism.

The Weimar Republic (1918 – 33) was encumbered by tremendous economic problems — brought on by post-war territorial losses, crippling reparation charges and the world depression — and by a flawed constitution which created a confused 'dual executive' consisting of a President, who was elected for a seven year term and who enjoyed significant plebiscitary and emergency powers, and a Chancellor — the intended chief executive officer — who required both the confidence of the lower house and the support of the President. This shared executive form of government was similar in many respects to that later adopted in the contemporary French Fifth Republic (1958- ). The key difference was in the electoral system, with the legislators of Weimar Germany being elected by a generous system of proportional representation which promoted the growth of a multitude of narrow splinter parties, each unable to obtain a governing majority, while Fifth Republic France has utilised a two-ballot 'run off' majority system. The Weimar period was thus one of coalition government and political instability, with fifteen Chancellors holding office between 1919 and 1933. In the final years of the Weimar Republic, power shifted away from the parties and the Chancellor towards the conservative President, Von Hindenberg (1847 – 1934), before Hitler's National Socialists gained power with 44% of the popular vote in January 1933 and proceeded to eliminate all significant opposition, pushing through an Enabling Act which granted Hitler full dictatorial powers in March 1933.

## The 1933 – 45 Nazi Era and Its Consequences

The rise to power of Adolf Hitler (1889 – 1945) and the events of 1933 - 45 have clouded all subsequent judgements of German politics. Many have viewed Nazism as a logical outcome of Germany's historical and economic development, with its weak bourgeoisie and failed revolutions, and the German national psyche, with its tradition of firm autocratic rule, statism, deference to authority and legendary discipline. In this interpretation, Germans, by nature, prefer direction from above and groupism to individualism and liberal democracy. Others have viewed the rise of Hitler as a chance development resulting from the specific economic circumstances of the early 1930s and his subsequent extreme nationalist and racist policies as unexpected aberrations. What is clear is that both the structural and economic circumstances of inter-war Germany provided, as in contemporary Italy, a fertile ground for fascism. Hitler did attract significant popular support, particularly from the north and Bavarian south of the nation, from Protestants, small towns, the lower middle classes, rural and marginal groups and the unemployed, and his remarkably successful interventionist and autarchic economic policies were a prime factor behind this popularity.

The Nazi regime proved in the end to be self-destructive, its expansionism meeting with increasing external resistance from the winter of 1942 as Soviet troops turned the tide at Stalingrad. The Third Reich finally collapsed in May 1945, following the suicide of Hitler as the Allies advanced upon Berlin, and the large German empire was thereafter dismembered. The eastern, Prussian, half was divided between Poland and the newly created Soviet satellite, the German Democratic Republic (GDR). Out of the larger western portion, the Federal Republic of Germany (FRG) was constructed. It was placed under temporary Allied rule between 1945 and 1949, as a new stable democratic system was devised.

Rebuilding began first at the provincial or state (*Land*) level, where political parties began operating in the interim period. Then in September 1948 Allied military governors met with provincial leaders and set up a 65-member constituent assembly to draft a new provisional constitution (the Basic Law; *Grundgesetz*), which was ratified by the *Länder* parliaments in May 1949.[1] This, 146 article, provisional document has survived to become the constitutional charter for the modern West German state. The chief concern of the architects of this document was to avoid the mistakes of the Weimar constitution and to prevent a revival of totalitarian Nazism. They aimed, firstly, at strengthening the authority of the Chancellor and the parliamentary parties vis-à-vis the President and the state bureaucracy and armed forces; secondly, at devolving significant powers to the provincial level; and thirdly, at establishing the supremacy of the law. A unique and unusually successful 'liberal-democratic' political system was thus created, borrowing from British, American and European precedents.

## The 1949 Constitution and Postwar Political System

### The strengthening of the Bundestag and the Chancellor

The powers of the President were drastically reduced in the Federal

---

[1] Bavaria was alone among Länder parliaments in May 1949 in voting against the Basic Law.

3

Republic after 1949. Instead of being directly elected by the public — as in the Weimar period — the President was now appointed, for a maximum of two five-year terms, by a Federal Convention (*Bundesversammlung*) composed of the members of the Bundestag and an equal number from the Länder assemblies. The President was thus destined to become just a party and parliamentary nominee (See Table 1) — a ceremonial figurehead, whose powers of intervention were unusually limited.[1] Instead, in the modern West German state, real power was transferred to the lower house of parliament — the *Bundestag* — and to the Chancellor (Prime Minister), who, through his political party, commanded a majority in this house.

#### Table 1   The Presidents of West Germany

| | Party | Age on Election | Term in Office |
|---|---|---|---|
| Theodor Heuss | FDP | 65 | 1949 – 1959 |
| Heinrich Lübke | CDU | 64 | 1959 – 1969 |
| Gustav Heinemann | SPD | 70 | 1969 – 1974 |
| Walter Scheel | FDP | 55 | 1974 – 1979 |
| Karl Carstens | CDU | 65 | 1979 – 1984 |
| Richard von Weizsäcker | CDU | 64 | 1984 – |

The new Bundestag was composed of 402 (today 497) deputies[2] elected at regular four year intervals[3] by a unique and complicated

[1] The Presidents selected since 1949 have usually been moderate, elderly, centrist figures, whose ability to influence the national debate on policy issues has varied with their individual personalities and national standing. The present President, Richard Von Weizsäcker, has been one of the most active and respected Presidents, delivering, in May 1985, on the fortieth anniversary of the ending of the Second World War, what has been recognised as one of the great speeches of postwar Germany,cautioning his fellow countrymen not to be complacent or forgetful about the nation's past and to guard against a revival in crude nationalist sentiment.

[2] This excludes the 22 'honorary deputies' from West Berlin who lack a federal vote (see Appendix D). It includes, however, one 'overhang' (*Uberhangmandat*) seat which was gained by a party winning more constituency (*Erststimmen*) seats in a Land than was indicated by its list vote. In such circumstances, which result from the uneven geographical distribution of a party's support within a Land, the party is entitled to retain all its Erststimmen seats and the Bundestag is accordingly increased in size. (At the 1980 election there was one Uberhangmandat seat, in 1983 two and in 1987 one).

[3] Elections can only be called midterm or more than several months before they are officially due in exceptional circumstances when a deadlock of power emerges in the Bundestag and the President is forced to grant a dissolution. In normal circumstances, however, West German governments, in contrast to British ones, are obliged to see out their full term and are unable to set their own date for opportune early elections.

system of 'personalised proportional representation'. Each adult was granted two votes, one — the *Erststimme* on the left side of the ballot paper — for a local constituency seat, the other — the *Zweitstimme* on the right side — for a party list covering his Land. Political parties were thus able to win seats both in the constituencies — from which 248 Bundestag members are now returned (being elected on a simple majority basis) — and within the Länder. The size of a party's list vote determined the final number of seats it would be entitled to from each region, with seats already gained at the constituency level being deducted from this proportionate number.

The Bundestag has been made the key legislative body in postwar West Germany. It elects and controls the federal government (ie. the Chancellor and his cabinet), selects one half of the members of the Federal Constitutional Court, and it supervises the work of the bureaucracy and armed forces. The Chancellor appoints a 16 − 20 member cabinet, taking account of the demands of party factions and coalition partners, and determines policy with the aid of a large, 400-member, specialist and supervisory private office. The Bundestag keeps a check on legislation through an increasingly vigorous system of 19 functional committees (each staffed by a chairman and 25 − 37 members drawn from Party *Fraktionen*[1] on a proportionate basis), through the use of a Westminster-style 'question hour', and through petitions for debates or inquiries. It is, however, only able to remove a Chancellor through a 'constructive vote of no-confidence', whereby a majority of delegates vote not only to reject the incumbent, but also positively in favour of a new Chancellor. This has been done successfully on only one occasion, in October 1982.

The actual authority of the Chancellor vis-à-vis his cabinet colleagues and the Bundestag has varied with the particular stature and personal qualities of each leader and the strength of his parliamentary party majority. During the period between 1949 and 1963 Konrad Adenauer (leader of the Christian Democratic Union — CDU) dominated German politics to such an extent that the term 'Chancellor Democracy' was invented — with the Chancellor governing in an unusually dominant, almost authoritarian, fashion and exerting control over his ministers in a manner akin to that of the US President. Since that date, however, with the rise of the Social

[1] Parties must form official groups or caucuses termed *Fraktionen* (sing. *Fraktion*) within the Bundestag, with the number of committee chairs and seats it is entitled to depending on its Fraktion size.

Democratic Party (SPD) party as an alternative governing party and with the regularisation of coalition government and the increased assertiveness of Bundestag deputies, the Chancellor's authority has shown signs of diminishing and the relationship between the Chancellor, the cabinet and elected chamber has moved closer to the British prime ministerial model. Between 1974 and 1982, there was a revival in the use of the term 'Chancellor Democracy', as Helmut Schmidt took decisive personal control over key sectors of federal government activity. Schmidt's successor as Chancellor, Helmut Kohl, has, however, been less assertive, leaving greater scope for policy making in the hands of individual, specialist cabinet ministers.[1]

## Federalism and regional checks

One distinguishing feature of the postwar German political system has been the devolution of significant powers to its constituent regions. Such devolution has been a consequence of the early regrowth of local democracy during the interim period between 1946 — 9 and of a desire to diffuse political power. It also, however, reflects the continuing strength of regionalist culture and sentiment which has resulted from Germany's long tradition of strong state-level government.

West Germany is today (exclusive of West Berlin: see Appendix D) composed of ten Länder, which vary substantially in size from the large states of Bavaria and North-Rhine-Westphalia, each with a population in excess of ten million, to the tiny city-states of Hamburg and Bremen (see Figure 1 and Appendix A). Each Land has its own miniature government headed by a minister-president and supported by an elected assembly, written constitution, and constitutional court.[2] These Länder parliaments (*Landtage*) have only a few original powers (mainly involving the police, local government, and education), but they, through their own sizeable civil services, are responsible for carrying out the administration of federal matters

---

[1] Cabinet ministers in West Germany do not need to be Bundestag deputies, although, usually nearly all are. This has enabled a number of technocrat experts, for example Manfred Lahnstein, who was finance minister in the Schmidt government of 1982, to be inducted into the ministerial team.

[2] The Länder legislatures are all single chamber bodies with the exception of bicameral Bavaria. In the city states of Bremen and West Berlin, the elected chief executive officer is termed a *Bürgermeister* (mayor) rather than minister-president.

(excluding defence, foreign policy and currency affairs) within their region.[1] They have thus discretion in implementing federal priorities and they have powers of taxation and a voice in the assignation of revenue. Thus whereas in Great Britain, for example, the local governments are responsible for only a quarter of total government spending and are dependent on the centre for a half of their revenue, in West Germany more than a half of government spending is carried out by the Länder, who receive their own sizeable shares of income tax and VAT and only a quarter of their revenue from Bonn. The significant powers held by Länder parliaments have meant that state elections have been hard-fought (with turnouts in excess of 70% — compared to 40% in Britain — and with contests being seen as important tests of national midterm popularity) and that Länder have attracted talented politicians using the state stage for subsequent entries into the higher levels of federal politics. The power wielded by Länder governments has also meant that federal ministers have been forced to compromise over programmes and enter into backroom agreements with Länder officials and that many federal policies — for example, economic reflation and the introduction of comprehensive education during the 1970s and privatisation and conservative economic liberalism during the 1980s — have been thwarted. In recent years, the public profile of the minister-presidents of the larger Länder has increased, with state leaders emerging as unusually assertive champions for their Land economy, establishing lobbying offices at the European Community headquarters at Strasbourg and Brussels and engaging in personal international diplomacy of their own.

The Länder have in addition been given, under the 1949 Basic Law, a powerful voice at the federal level in Bonn in the second chamber of government, the *Bundesrat* (Federal Council). This upper house consists of 41 voting delegates sent and instructed by Länder governments. The four largest regions send five delegates, the three intermediate Länder, four delegates, and the three smallest Länder, three delegates (see Appendix A).[2] This system favours the small Länder, with Bremen, for example, sending one delegate per 224,000 people, compared to North-Rhine-Westphalia's one delegate per 3.4 million citizens. Delegates are chosen by ruling

---

[1] In 1980, the Länder governments employed 1.5 million workers and the lower tier county (*Kreise*) and municipal (*Gemeinden*) authorities 0.9 million. In comparison, the federal government employed 305,000. For this reason, federal ministries in West Germany are smaller and less powerful bodies than British central ministries.

[2] West Berlin sends four non-voting delegates to the Bundesrat.

Länder parties and vote in blocs — opposition parties in regions not being represented. The Bundesrat has no real powers of initiating legislation but it forms an important constitutional check with three main spheres of influence. Firstly, all legislation which directly relates to Länder responsibilities requires Bundesrat approval — more than 60% of Bundestag bills fall into this category today. Secondly, a two-thirds majority in the Bundesrat (as well as in the Bundestag) is required for constitutional amendments.[1] Thirdly, on other matters the Bundesrat can suggest amendments to Bundestag legislation, send disputed items to a 'joint conciliation committee' (*Vermittlungsausschuss*) drawn equally from both houses, and can temporarily block bills until a countervailing vote of either 50% or 66% in the Bundestag is passed.[2]

The Bundesrat holds plenary sessions for voting on legislation only once a month. The remainder of its work is effected in committees which are staffed by senior Länder civil servants who are allowed to deputise for their Länder ministers and minister-presidents. Despite this complexion, however, the political nature and importance of the Bundesrat has increased in recent years. In particular, during the 1970s the CDU, enjoying a Bundesrat majority, used the body to block and delay Bundestag legislation passed by the dominant SPD-FDP coalition. In an attempt to place restrictions upon such activities, the Federal Constitutional Court decided in 1974 that new Bundestag legislation which merely amended statutes which had already been passed by the Bundesrat would no longer require further upper house approval. Despite this ruling, however, the indirectly elected Bundesrat has remained an influential and controversial body. Such is the continued strength of regional power in the West German polity that federal politicians have recently been seeking its reduction to facilitate policy co-ordination in an increasingly complex modern society. This contrasts with the movement against excessive centralisation experienced in neighbouring Western democracies.

[1] There have been more than thirty amendments to the Basic Law since 1949. The most important, which were introduced between 1954 − 6 and 1966 − 9, were concerned with the new federal armed forces and defining the extent of emergency powers.

[2] A 50% Bundestag countervailing vote is required for bills rejected by a simple majority in the Bundesrat; a 66% vote for bills rejected by a two-thirds majority of seats upper house. In addition, if the opposition parties gain a two-thirds majority of seats within the Bundesrat they are entitled to veto **all** legislation passed on from the Bundestag and the federal governing party/coalition would need to muster regular 66% majorities of its own in the lower house to see through its legislation.

**The rule of law**

A second check and balance was built into the German political system through the creation of a written constitution (the Basic Law) and the establishment of the Federal Constitutional Court as a policing body.

West Germany, like other continental countries, had inherited a codified legal system, influenced by Roman practice, in which judges acted merely as neutral executioners and administrators even during the excesses of the 1933 − 45 Third Reich. This contrasted with the judge-made and interpreted law of Britain and the United States. The Allied occupying powers were anxious to move closer towards the latter system through granting certain courts the power of judicial review. They thus set up, at Karlsruhe, the Federal Constitutional Court (*Bundesverfassungsgericht*) to act as final arbiter in constitutional questions and as the guarantor of civil liberties.

This court, which is independently financed, is composed of sixteen judges, qualified in law and appointed for a twelve year, non-renewable term. Half of these judges are selected by the Bundesrat and half by the Bundestag. They are each nominated by a balanced selection committee and require a two-thirds majority of support — a fair balance of different party representatives is thus ensured, with extremists being excluded by the 66% rule. The Court is responsible for ensuring that Länder rights are upheld, that the correct balance is maintained between federal and Länder interests, that government organs act constitutionally, and that the individual civil rights set out in Articles 1 - 19 of the Basic Law — the freedoms of speech, assembly, association, security and choice of employment — are maintained. Opposition politicians in the Bundestag can thus use the body to challenge legislation on the grounds of constitutional legality. The Constitutional Court is held in high regard by the German public and, although subject to political appointment and less confident and 'activist' than the United States' Supreme Court, has not been afraid on occasion to controversially overturn federal decisions.

## Political Stability and Mature Democracy

The checks and balances created by the Basic Law have been remarkably successful in creating a popular and stable democratic system during the decades since 1949. There have been only six different Chancellors during the last 38 years of the Fourth Reich and two major political parties have dominated the parliamentary arena. Although foreign observers have constantly sought to uncover the evidence of cracks in German democracy and have anticipated a lurch back towards autocracy, postwar German politics has, in comparison to French, Italian or British, been unusually tranquil and consensual. This has fed through to the German economy which has enjoyed more than three decades of unparalleled growth and prosperity. The creation of a strong 'party-state' controlled by two sensible, modern political parties has been the key ingredient during this harmonious era.

## The party state

Germany's political parties had opposed Nazism, before they were themselves outlawed in 1933. They were thus seen as the true bastions of democracy around which the new German polity should be constructed. The framers of the Basic Law, therefore, gave a special role to the new parties in 'forming the political will of the people'. They thus introduced, for example, state financing of parties and extended the authority of parties over the bureaucracy (now staffed at its upper levels by party members), military and judiciary — groups who had been dangerously independent during the Imperial and Weimar periods. Such has been the all-pervading influence of postwar German political parties that West Germany has been termed a 'party-state' (*Parteienstaat*). This state has been dominated by two major parties, the CDU and SPD, who have held political power for 22 and 13 years respectively during the period between 1949 and 1987, and who jointly held power in coalition between 1966 and 1969. A third minor party, the Free Democratic Party (FDP), has participated in coalition governments with each of these two parties for 31 of these 38 years. (See Table 2).

**Table 2    Federal Governments in West Germany 1949 – 87**

|  | Coalition Parties | Chancellor |
|---|---|---|
| 1949 - 1963 | CDU - CSU, FDP[1] | Adenauer |
| 1963 - 1966 | CDU - CSU, FDP | Erhard |
| 1966 - 1969 | CDU - CSU, SPD | Kiesinger |
| 1969 - 1974 | SPD, FDP | Brandt |
| 1974 - 1982 | SPD, FDP | Schmidt |
| 1982 - | CDU - CSU, FDP | Kohl |

[1] Also involved in the coalition between 1949 - 61 were the DP German Party and, between 1953 -7, the BHE expellees party. The FDP left the coalition between 1957 and 1961.

Such party dominance has been unusual. During the Imperial and Weimar era Germany had been famed for its weak and diffuse party system. More than a dozen political parties vied for power, with half of these gaining significant electoral support. This profusion of political parties was a consequence of both the late and uneven economic development of pre-war Germany and of its electoral system.

The economic and social revolution wrought by the Nazi era and the constitutional innovations of 1949 overcame these barriers to political maturity. The Nazi and wartime period first speeded up the pace of industrial development and urbanisation and removed traditionalist elites — reducing all groups to the same level and bequeathing a dissevered nation in 1945. This essentially destructive period paradoxically helped modernise the German nation, providing the flattened and, with the loss of East Germany, homogenous base from which the successful Fourth Reich could be constructed anew, and it provided an environment in which new broadly based, non-sectional, 'catch-all' parties could later flourish. Continuing industrialisation and urbanisation during the postwar decades and the constitutional changes of 1949 reinforced this shift away from diffusion to concentration in the party system. The most significant constitutional innovations were Article 21 Section 2, which granted the Constitutional Court the power to ban extremist anti-democratic political parties (this was used in 1952 against the neo-Nazi SRP, and in 1956 against the communist KPD), and the changes made in the electoral rules.

During the Weimar period an extreme pure proportional representation system operated in which the country was divided up into 35 giant constituencies and where it was possible for local regionalist parties to win seats with barely 0.2% of the national vote. The framers of the 1949 constitution introduced, by contrast, the 'personalised proportional representation' system built around 248 individual constituencies (with an average today of 240,000 voters each) and a parallel Länder list. It was a compromise between the British and American 'first-past-the-post' and the Weimar list systems and was buttressed by the additional rule introduced in 1956 that a party would need to win more than 5% of the federal vote in order to qualify for seats. (Between 1953 and 1956 the 5% clause applied only to the Land vote). This change precipitated the demise during the early 1950s of minor regionally-based parties, such as the Bavarian Party, the right-wing northern Protestant, Lower Saxony-based, German Party and the BHE expellees party; it also propelled the movement towards a three party state with the CDU and SPD dominating, yet unable to gain a full Bundestag majority, and with the FDP acting as a crucial 'hinge' party and coalition partner. In 1949 these three principal parties gained 72% of the total federal vote, in 1957 90% and in 1976 99% (see Table 3). Only since 1978 with the rise of the ecological Green Party as a second significant minor party has a crack appeared in what has been termed the 'two-and-a-half party system).

Table 3    Party Shares of Bundestag Election Votes, 1949 – 1987
(% Of Zweitstimmen List Vote)

|  | 1949 | 1953 | 1957 | 1961 | 1965 | 1969 |
|---|---|---|---|---|---|---|
| CDU - CSU | 31.0 | 45.2 | 50.2 | 45.3 | 47.6 | 46.1 |
| SPD | 29.1 | 28.8 | 31.8 | 36.2 | 39.3 | 42.7 |
| FDP | 11.9 | 9.5 | 7.7 | 12.8 | 9.5 | 5.8 |
| GREENS | — | — | — | — | — | — |
| Electoral Turnout | 78.5% | 85.8% | 87.7% | 87.7% | 86.8% | 86.7% |

|  | 1972 | 1976 | 1980 | 1983 | 1987 |
|---|---|---|---|---|---|
| CDU - CSU | 44.9 | 48.6 | 44.5 | 48.8 | 44.3 |
| SPD | 45.8 | 42.6 | 42.9 | 38.2 | 37.0 |
| FDP | 8.4 | 7.9 | 10.6 | 6.9 | 9.1 |
| GREENS | — | — | 1.5 | 5.6 | 8.3 |
| Electoral Turnout | 91.1% | 90.7% | 87.8% | 89.1% | 84.4% |

## The Christian Democratic Union (CDU)

The CDU dominated West German politics and government during the first two decades of the Fourth Reich and it has remained the single most popular political party throughout the postwar era. The roots of the CDU went back to the Catholic Party of the Imperial period (set up to protect Catholic rights) and the Centre Party, which played a prominent role in the coalitions of the Weimar era. However, the postwar CDU, while still centred around a core of church-going Catholic support, became a far broader alliance of both centre-left and centre-right Protestants and Catholics who had resisted National Socialism and who set out now to defend the new postwar liberal democratic and anti-Soviet West German state.

The CDU benefited from the division of Germany — which resulted in the loss of radical Protestant, socialist-orientated areas to the new GDR — and was able to firmly establish itself in the large rural, Catholic Länder of southern and western Germany (Bavaria, Rhineland-Palatinate and Baden-Württemberg) and in rural

Protestant Schleswig-Holstein and Lower Saxony. With its strong Länder base, the CDU emerged as the largest single federal party in 1949 and came to permanently dominate the Bundesrat. During the 1950s support for the party expanded rapidly as the CDU absorbed minor regional and centre-right parties, gained a further support base in the industrialised Catholic Saar (which was restored to the Federal Republic in 1957) and successfully presided over the economic and political rejuvenation of Germany. The CDU integrated West Germany into NATO (1955) and the new European Community (1957), while at home their economics expert, Ludwig Erhard (Minister for Economic Affairs, 1949 - 63), devised a new economic policy, the 'social market economy' (*Soziale Marktwirtschaft*), which proved to be the ruling philosophy for the successful postwar German state. Under this formula, free-market forces were encouraged and income inequalities tolerated, while the government was left to 'steer' the economy in a socially responsible fashion — reconciling the interests of capital and labour, guarding against the formation of dangerous monopolies and providing the infra-structure of a modern welfare state. This policy proved to be a great success and helped to win over to the CDU new blue and white-collar secular groups, converting it into a broad-church *Volkspartei*, with, by the 1970s, 35% of its support being drawn from the industrial workforce.

With such an electoral combination, the CDU was able to gain near majorities in the Bundestag between 1949 and 1966, governing with the support of the liberal FDP, and to control the majority of Länder and hence the Bundesrat. The hold of the CDU began to weaken, however, during the mid-1960s. Its rival for political power, the SPD, came to terms with contemporary conditions, changing its policies accordingly, while at the same time offering attractive new initiatives, most notably Ostpolitik. At the same time, the CDU faced increasing internal problems. It had become too tied to the personally popular Adenauer and failed to strengthen its organisation to give its leader greater control over its powerful Länder chiefs. Thus the CDU's subsequent chairmen — Ludwig Erhard (1963 - 6), Kurt Kiesinger (1966 - 70), Rainer Barzel (1970 - 3) and Helmut Kohl (1973 - ) — found it increasingly difficult to control what became a decentralised and faction-riven party (highlighted by the machinations of its right-wing Catholic offshoot in Bavaria, the Christian Social Union (CSU), led by Franz-Josef Strauss). Support for the CDU remained solid during the 1960s and early 1970s at between 45 - 48% of the electorate, but the SPD's vote increased significantly from 30% to almost 45% during the corresponding period, forcing coalition government in 1966, before the SPD, in combination with the FDP, eventually took over as the governing party in 1969. This left the CDU with only its Länder bases and Bundesrat majority to attempt to block unpalatable reforms.

## The Social Democratic Party (SPD)

The SPD replaced the CDU as the party of government in 1969 and remained in power for the next thirteen years. This party boasted a venerable political history dating back to the Bismarckian era (having been founded in 1875 at Gotha), with its early support being derived from industrial areas in response to a programme with strong Marxist leanings. On the eve of the First World War, the SPD had one million members and it became the major political party during the Weimar period, forming governments in 1919 - 20 and 1928 - 30. The policy stance of the SPD became more moderate during the 1920s, following the 1917 breakaway of the extremist USPD wing (later KPD) and the crushing of the Spartakus revolution in 1919. The SPD maintained a leadership in exile during the Nazi era and expected to sweep the election in 1949, but they were weakened by the loss of many bastions of support in East Germany and by the populist shift in the CDU programme. The party thus remained excluded from federal government until 1966. It did, however, control the state parliaments in the industrialised Länder of Hamburg, Hesse, Bremen and the Rhine-Ruhr belt of North-Rhine-Westphalia.

During the early postwar years the SPD, led by Kurt Schumacher (1949 − 52) and Erich Ollenhauer (1952 − 61), pursued a political programme radically opposed to that of the CDU and refused to engage in coalitions. They pressed for economic planning and nationalisation, and opposed European integration and re-armanent. It became clear, however, after the 1957 Bundestag election, when Konrad Adenauer gained an absolute majority of the votes, that a radical change in policies would be required if the SPD was to break out of its '30% ghetto' and attract sufficient white-collar and middle class support to form a future government. A campaign for reform was thus instigated by key figures within the SPD — Willy Brandt (the new mayor of West Berlin), Herbert Wehner (later the party's parliamentary Fraktion leader), Karl Schiller (its economics expert) and Helmut Schmidt. Their aim was to modernise the party and bring it into line with the changed circumstances of the postwar era of economic growth, political integration and changing social structures — with the increase in personal mobility, the expansion in the white-collar service sector, the decline in traditional class-based and religious allegiances, and the 'embourgeoisement' of the population. This campaign bore fruit at the party conference in Bad Godesberg in 1959, when a fundamental re-definition of Social Democracy was approved — disavowing the party's traditional Marxist connections, class orientation and anti-clericalism, and accepting the new 'social market economy' and membership of NATO and the EEC. The SPD thus moved very close to the programme of the CDU, though showing a greater concern for social equality and a greater willingness to intervene and manage the economy.

With the adoption of this programme and the election of the charismatic Willy Brandt as chancellor-candidate in 1961 and party chairman in 1964, support for the SPD steadily increased during the 1960s. The party first tasted power in 1966, when, after the FDP had withdrawn support from the existing administration, the SPD joined forces with the CDU in a 'Grand Coalition' between 1966 and 1969. This provided an opportunity for the SPD to prove themselves responsible and effective custodians of office, and the opportunity was grasped, with the SPD's economics minister, Karl Schiller, proving particularly adept at rescuing West Germany from the economic recession of 1966. This bore dividends in 1969, when a significant advance in the party's electoral support was recorded.

The SPD became the ruling party in the Bundestag between 1969 and 1982 (being led first by Willy Brandt between 1969 − 74 and then by the pragmatic Helmut Schmidt between 1974 − 82), partly as a result of this broadening in its electoral appeal and of contemporary demographic movements (the rise in the proportion of younger voters and male voters — a traditionally more radical psephological group), but also as a result of the changing coalition tactics of Germany's third principal party, the FDP. Although the SPD's share of the Bundestag vote rose to above 40% during the elections between 1969 and 1976, only in 1972 did its total vote exceed that of the CDU (see Table 3). It was the additional 6 - 10% of electoral support provided by the FDP which allowed the SPD to put together governing majorities.

## The Free Democratic Party (FDP)

The FDP, the heir of the ill-fated German liberal tradition, has been the crucial 'pivot' party around which the modern coalition system has rotated. The party has constantly held the balance of power and although receiving only 10% or less of the popular vote, the FDP has captured over 20% of ministerial portfolios during the Fourth Reich and acted as a significant moderating force. Prior to 1966 the FDP, though obstensibly a liberal and non-sectarian party, allied itself with the conservative CDU: between 1969 and 1982 it formed regular pacts with the SPD, threatening to permanently squeeze the CDU out of federal power. Two factors explained this switch in allegiance — the moderation in the SPD policy programme following Bad Godesberg, and the progressivist shift in the FDP's stance, following the election of Walter Scheel as party chairman in 1968. The FDP had during the 1950s been dominated by marginal farming groups and by small town conservatives. However, during the mid 1960s its more radical wing, centred in Baden-Württemberg in the southwest and in Hamburg and Bremen, gained a stronger voice as the party now orientated itself more towards white-collar groups. The party, also attracted by Willy Brandt's espousal of conciliatory *Ostpolitik* and seeking to avoid absorption by the CDU, thus abandoned its pact with the CDU in 1966 and formed a new partnership with the SPD in 1969. In return, the FDP were granted four significant ministries (foreign affairs, interior, agriculture and, after 1974, economics) in a cabinet of thirteen. In addition, the party's leader Walter Scheel was made federal President in 1974 and his successor Hans-Dietrich Genscher was appointed foreign minister and Vice Chancellor.

## Political Maturity and Consensus Politics

West German politics have been distinguished by a remarkable degree of political stability during the period since 1949, with two major parties dominating, but with, as a result of its electoral system, coalition governments — invariably involving the FDP — having been the rule. The two principal parties, while retaining specific core areas of support (the CDU — church-going Catholics, rural groups, South Germans and the elderly: the SPD — industrial workers, urban areas and the young) and while still differing in philosophy and policy orientation, have converged to an unusual degree. They now compete strongly to win the fickle allegiance of the well-educated, often white-collar, modern 'classless' voter, the support of whom is crucial in the quest for political power. West Germany has thus become a mature democracy with peaceful and increasingly regular alternations in governments and with a high degree of popular participation — Bundestag election turnouts have averaged 87 – 91% compared to 70–75% in Britain.

West German political parties have become geared to an unusual extent towards the acquisition and retention of this power, rather than ideological squabbles. Principled opposition has become rare; instead coalition pacts are made in advance and, once in government, the Chancellor has remained in office for his four year term — scandals and unusual crises aside — unable, as for example in Britain, to seek an advantageous early dissolution. The absence of midterm Bundestag by-elections (vacant seats being filled by unsuccessful candidates next on the party list), and the fact that an unusually high proportion of German politicians are civil servants by background and that ministers are skilled, specialist technocrats, has added to the administrative, rather than adversarial nature of modern West German politics — a form of politics concerned with utilising rather than arguing over the acquisition of power.[1] Such a corporatist, consensual approach to politics is evident, above all, in the economic field with the co-operative, 'social-market' *Konzertierte Aktion* strategy of the government and the trade-union and managerial interest groups enshrined in the 1967 'Stability Law', which has been an important factor behind the postwar German 'economic miracle'.

Paradoxically, it has been Germany's past history of fragile, insecure political democracy, coupled with the destruction of traditional power bases wrought by the Nazi Third Reich and the Second World War, which has proved advantageous in the construction of a successful liberal democratic system during the postwar era. A new constitution and political system has been framed afresh, learning from past mistakes and from the experience of other democracies. Checks and balances have been built into a constitution which divides power between the centre and the regions, forcing compromise and co-operation between Bonn and the constituent states. New modern 'catch all' *Volksparteien* have developed largely free from the class and interest group ties which

---

[1] In West Germany, unlike in Britain or the United States, a civil servant is not debarred from holding legislative office. Instead, he/she is granted six weeks paid leave while fighting a campaign and, if elected, is allowed a leave of absence during the term of office. Selection of half the Bundestag through the list system also facilitates the election of skilled bureaucrats who may have lacked the political wiles to have succeeded through a direct hustings route. By the mid-1970s, surveys showed that around 44% of Bundestag deputies were former public employees and 25% were officials of interest groups.

have encumbered political parties in neighbouring European countries and have been led by responsible, moderate-minded leaders. From this base, a successful consensual and corporatist economic and political system has emerged, with integration into the European Community solidifying and underpinning this democratic stability. However, despite these achievements, not all groups have been satisfied with the 'Fourth and Richest Reich'. For a number of citizens there remains a lack of roots, ideals, purpose and radicalism in the Fourth Reich. Such feelings have been reflected in the campaigns for German re-unification, in the 1970s urban terrorist movement and, more recently, in the rise of the ecologist Green Party. Even more serious problems have been presented by the economic recession and the new 'cold war' of the 1980s, which has seriously undermined Germany's post-1959 political consensus, creating serious divisions over defence and economic strategies between the CDU-CSU and the SPD. The following pages examine such developments during a decade of uncertainty and change.

# Part Two

# POLITICAL DEVELOPMENTS: 1976-1987

## 1969-75: SPD-FDP Dominance — CDU Re-Appraisal

The SPD-FDP coalition replaced the CDU in 1969 and continued in office for a further 13 years. This *Machtwechsel* (change of power) ushered in a new and more reformist era in which Chancellor Brandt declared his willingness to 'risk more democracy', improve social justice and encourage greater participation in the political arena. The voting age was lowered to 18 (in 1972), industrial co-determination (*Mitbestimmung*) was introduced, the educational system was reformed and expanded, and welfare spending on the young, elderly and handicapped was increased significantly. In the economic sphere, there was now greater state involvement in medium- and short-term planning and a more concerted use of fiscal policy in a Keynesian fashion. In foreign affairs, improved relations with the East were encouraged through Ostpolitik. During this period the SPD was led by a strong, united and experienced team centred around the troika of party chairman Willy Brandt, parliamentary floor leader Herbert Wehner and, from May 1974, the popular, skilled and highly respected Chancellor Helmut Schmidt. The image presented and marketed was one of sensible, pragmatic, responsible reformism led by a new generation of postwar politicians.

These policies and this approach reaped rich electoral dividends for the SPD during the early 1970s, as the party matched the changing social tenor of the times. New educated white collar groups, some of whom had been involved in the APO (Extra-Parliamentary) student movement of 1966−9, were now attracted to the SPD, in addition to its more traditional blue-collar and middle class constituency. This was reflected by the increase in SPD party membership from 710 000 in 1965 to 998 000 in 1975 and by its electoral performance in the 1972 Bundestag contest, when it became the largest national-level single party for the first time ever. The relationship between the SPD and FDP coalition partners was also placed on a more formal and legitimate footing during this period with the introduction of the 'new rules' of 1972. From this date on, coalition preferences and pacts were to be made openly before the date of the election, with both parties pledging to maintain the arrangement throughout the ensuing legislative term.

19

Greater solidity was thus given to the governments of these years and the door was left open for split, tactical voting — in which constituency votes would be given to the SPD and list votes to the FDP — in the Bundestag elections of 1972–80, to the benefit of the coalition ticket. In such circumstances, despite predictions of its imminent demise, the FDP continued to surmount the 5% electoral hurdle and acted as a moderating check upon more extreme elements within the SPD.

The CDU, by contrast, was driven into the federal wilderness during the 1970s. It retained, however, considerable electoral support and continued to dominate the majority of Länder and the Bundersrat, and was thus able to exert pressure to indirectly influence SPD policy programmes. This checked any tendencies there may have been towards the party's disintegration. Instead, the CDU used these years in exile to carry out fundamental party re-organisation and to reformulate and re-define its policy approach and public image.

During the 1950s and early 1960s, under Konrad Adenauer and Ludwig Erhard, the CDU had presented the appearance of a loose confederation of regional chiefs coming together every four years to choose and support an agreed chancellor-candidate. The central organisation of the party had been limited and ineffectual, thus regional cleavages rapidly emerged once out of office. Recognising these weaknesses, the CDU's chairmen of the early 1970s, Rainer Barzel (1970–3) and Helmut Kohl (1973–    ), and its general-secretary, Kurt Biedenkopf, set about strengthening the central party apparatus (a new headquarters, the Konrad Adenauer House, being constructed at Bonn), establishing new 'wings' to attract targetted support and improving inter-Länder integration. This remodelling programme met with considerable success, CDU membership increasing dramatically from only 300 000 in 1970 to 696 000 in 1980 (membership of the Bavarian CSU increased during the same period from 118 000 to 175 000), and established in place a potentially more efficient structure for mobilising the paty's federal vote in future Bundestag elections. Secondly, the policy stance of the CDU was re-developed under the leadership of the moderate-minded Helmut Kohl. The party thus now came to terms with Willy Brandt's Ostpolitik detente and shifted to the centre in its economic and domestic policy approach, though continuing to favour greater fiscal probity than the Keynesian SPD. This did not add up to a transformation of Bad Godesberg proportions, but the changes remained substantial and served to make the CDU more attractive to the floating 'middle ground' centrist voter, as well as opening the door once more to an alliance with the FDP, which would be crucial if the party was to recover federal power once again.

## 1976—79: CDU Abortive Recovery

The tide of public opinion moved away from the ruling SPD during the mid-1970s as economic problems mounted and as the impetus fizzled out of Ostpolitik detente. The West German economy, following five years of robust recovery from the 1966—7 recession, spluttered during the mid—1970s as a result of the quadrupling of world oil prices by OPEC in 1973—4. The resulting slowdown in world economic growth pushed unemployment in the heavily export-orientated West German economy to over one million and created public spending and inflationary pressures as the cost of the social welfare programmes of the early 1970s continued to increase. Chancellor Schmidt dealt with these problems more successfully than other Western leaders, but the onset of recession still brought benefits to the CDU-CSU in the October 1976 Bundestag election. Led by Helmut Kohl, the successful minister-president of the Rhineland-Palatinate, and campaigning under the slogans of "Freedom in place of Socialism" and "Less power for the State", the CDU reversed the electoral trend of the last decade. Support for the SPD declined for the first time since 1953 (the SPD losing a million votes to its rivals) and the CDU recaptured its pre-eminence as the largest single federal party once more, with the SPD-FDP's Bundestag majority being sliced from 46 to a mere 10 seats (see Table 4). The CDU gained an absolute majority (54%) of direct mandates for the first time since 1965 and captured 48.6% of 'list votes', its second best ever result. Indeed, with a single-ballot, 'first-past-the-post' British or American style electoral system it would have gained a large and comfortable parliamentary majority. However, despite being narrowly excluded from office once more by the German PR list system, the CDU seemed destined to grasp full control in 1980, if economic conditions deteriorated further.

The CDU failed, however, to capitalise on this situation. Instead, it fell prey to serious internal divisions during the three years following the October 1976 Bundestag election. Helmut Kohl left Land politics immediately after the federal election and moved to Bonn to become CDU-CSU Bundestag Fraktion leader in an effort to gain greater experience on the federal stage. Kohl, however, encountered increasing criticism and damaging opposition from Franz-Josef Strauss, the experienced and energetic leader of the

21

CSU sister party, who possessed a firm political base in the large, strongly Catholic state of Bavaria.[1] The clash between Kohl and Strauss precipitated the most serious internal crisis in the CDU-CSU coalition since 1950.

**Table 4   The October 1976 Bundestag Election**
(Turnout 90.7%)

|  | ('000) Zweitstimmen Votes | (%) Share of Total Vote | Seats |
|---|---|---|---|
| SPD | 16 099 | 42.6 | 214 |
| CDU | 14 367 | 38.0 | 190 |
| CSU | 4 027 | 10.6 | 53 |
| FDP | 2 995 | 7.9 | 39 |
| DKP | 118 | 0.3 | 0 |
| NPD | 123 | 0.3 | 0 |
| KBW* | 20 | 0.1 | 0 |
| Others | 72 | 0.2 | 0 |
| TOTAL | 37 821 | 100.0 | 496 |

*The Communist League of West Germany
(A Maoist organisation which was disbanded in 1980).

Strauss and the CSU were, in policy terms, far to the right of the larger CDU. They were strongly committed to individualism and liberal free-market economics and in foreign affairs were firmly Atlanticist and anti-communist — opposing one-sided detente. Strauss thus wished to move the CDU away from the consensual moderation preached by Helmut Kohl back towards the conservatism of Konrad Adenauer, adding to this a dash of Germanic and Bavarian nationalism and his own aggressive and confrontational personality. He had contested for the CDU-CSU chancellor candidacy in 1976, but had been defeated by Helmut Kohl. He vowed thereafter to plot his downfall and to replace Kohl as CDU-CSU chancellor-candidate in 1980.

[1] Strauss, born in Munich in 1915, had served for thirty years in the Bundestag between 1949-78, holding the offices of minister without portfolio (1953-5), minister of nuclear energy (1955-6) and minister of defence (1956-62) in the administrations of Konrad Adenauer. His federal career suffered a severe setback, however, in 1962 when he was forced to resign as defence minister following the 'Spiegel affair' in which he sanctioned illegal police raids of the *Der Spiegel* newspaper offices in Hamburg and Bonn as a result of its publication of critical reports on West Germany's defence policy. Strauss returned to federal administration between 1966-9, serving as finance minister in Kiesinger's 'Grand Coalition' government. From the 1960s, however, he concentrated increasingly on Bavarian issues, having become chairman of the CSU in 1961.

Strauss's criticisms of Kohl's allegedly weak and ineffective leadership intensified after the 1976 federal election, and at a meeting held at Wildrab-Kreuth in November 1976 the CSU delegation voted to end its 26 year old agreement to form a common voting caucus (*Fraktionsgemeinschaft*) with the CDU in the Bundestag. This threatened to precipitate a full schism between the CDU and CSU, with the CDU contesting seats in Bavaria and the CSU setting itself up as a federal-wide fourth party. The CSU, however, aware of the electoral perils of such a policy, pulled itself back from the brink in December 1976, renewing its parliamentary agreement in return for a number of concessions which gave the CSU Bundestag group greater freedom of action. Relations between the sister parties remained, however, strained.

Following the October 1978 Land election, Franz-Josef Strauss resigned his Bundestag seat and left Bonn to become minister-president of Bavaria. He continued, however, to criticise Kohl's federal leadership and pushed himself forward once again as chancellor-candidate. Strauss gained the support of conservative CDU leaders from the southern and central states of Baden-Württemberg and Hesse. Northern liberals' (*'Nordlichter'*) and moderates (including Kohl) within the CDU sought to foil Strauss's challenge by promoting the candidacy of the popular minister-president of Lower Saxony, Ernst Albrecht, as a compromise 'unity candidate'. They acted too late, however, and in July 1979 Franz-Josef Strauss was elected as the joint CDU-CSU chancellor-candidate for the October 1980 federal election. This choice was to prove disastrous for the Christian Democrats.

The SPD by contrast, following a lull in their electoral fortunes during the mid-1970s, gained in strength during the late 1970s as a result of the increasing popularity of their leader Helmut Schmidt. Schmidt, born in December 1918, the son of a middle class Hamburg schoolmaster, had distinguished himself as a Lieutenant and battery commander in the *Wehrmacht* (the Germany Third Reich army) on the Russian front during the Second World War, being awarded an Iron Cross. Unlike Adenauer or Brandt, Schmidt had not been an active opponent of Nazism, serving instead as a loyal and apolitical defender and servant of the nation. However, during his period as a prisoner of war between April and August 1945 he began to reflect on the Nazi experience and gained a new political awareness and concern for social justice. After the war, Schmidt took a degree in economics at Hamburg University, studying under the supervision of Karl Schiller, joined the radical

Social Democratic Student Movement (SDS) and SPD, and began work in the Hamburg city economics and transport department. He moved to Bonn in 1953, serving as an SPD Bundestag 'list delegate', and gained an early reputation as a left-wing socialist who favoured pacifism and greater nationalisation. By the time of the SPD's November 1959 Bad Godesberg conference, however, he had reformulated his views, emerging as a moderate, centrist 'social democrat'. Schmidt returned to his native Hamburg in 1961 to take up the position of minister of internal affairs and established a national reputation for himself as a result of his decisive handling of a serious flood crisis in February 1962. Benefiting from this experience, he was promoted to the post of SPD shadow defence minister in the Bundestag in 1965 and was appointed party 'floor leader' during the 1967–9 'Grand Coalition'.

Schmidt gained the reputation during his first twenty years in public service as both a hard-working and efficient administrator, with a fine grasp of details and broader strategy, and as a tough, caustic and persuasive debater. His two fields of particular expertise were defence strategy (writing the well received books *Defence or Reprisal* and *The Balance of Power* in 1961 and 1971) and economic management. During the 1969-74 Brandt administration, Schmidt thus successively headed the key federal defence (1969–72) and finance (1972–4) ministries. He was also appointed SPD Deputy Chairman in 1968. This was a clear indication that Schmidt was being groomed by Brandt for future party and national leadership. His accession to the Chancellorship in May 1974, following Brandt's resignation over the Guillaume spy scandal, however, came earlier than either leader had expected.

In contrast to the unpredictable, romantic and visionary Brandt, Schmidt was a pragmatic, non-ideological politician concerned with practical solutions — 'Realpolitik' — rather than with theory. By the early 1970s he was situated on the moderate, *Kanalarbeiter* ('channel workers') right wing of the SPD and enjoyed extensive personal contacts with industrialists and senior figures from all sides of the German political spectrum. He ascended to the Chancellorship as the most well-prepared and technically accomplished of postwar West German leaders and further strengthened his authority by gathering together a large and high-powered team of personal Chancellery advisers — Hans Jürgen Wischnewski (party liaison officer and political troubleshooter); Klaus Bölling (government spokesman); Manfred Schüler (head of the Chancellery, 1974–80); Manfred Lahnstein (head of the Chancellery 1980-2);

Horst Schulmann (in charge of the economics department); and Jorgen Ruhfus and Otto der Gablentz (foreign policy advisers). These aides briefed the voracious new Chancellor on all major policy initiatives and engaged in exhausting brain-storming discussions before an agreed policy was hammered out which Schmidt would then proceed to persuasively 'sell' to his ministerial colleagues.

## Table 5 The Schmidt Administration Cabinet of February 1978[1]

| Helmut Schmidt | SPD | Federal Chancellor |
|---|---|---|
| Hans-Dietrich Genscher | FDP | Vice-Chancellor & Foreign Affairs |
| Dr Otto Graf Lambsdorf | FDP | Economic Affairs |
| Prof. Werner Maihofer | FDP | Interior |
| Hans Matthöfer | SPD | Finance |
| Dr Hans-Jöchen Vogel | SPD | Justice |
| Dr Hans Apel | SPD | Defence |
| Josef Ertl | FDP | Food, Agriculture & Forestry |
| Dr Herbert Ehrenberg | SPD | Labour & Social Affairs |
| Kurt Gscheidle | SPD | Transport, Posts & Telecommunications |
| Dr Dieter Haack | SPD | Housing & Town Planning |
| Egon Franke | SPD | Inter-German Affairs |
| Dr Jürgen Schmude | SPD | Education & Science |
| Dr Volker Hauff | SPD | Research & Technology |
| Rainer Offergeld | SPD | Economic Co-operation |
| Frau Antje Huber | SPD | Youth, Family & Health |

[1] The Schmidt cabinets of 1974-82 were unusually young, with an average age of below 50, containing a new generation of postwar technocrats.

Although constrained by the realities of coalition government (see Table 5) and by the federal system, Chancellor Schmidt was able to make a firm imprint upon the direction taken by the government during the years between 1974 and 1980. He pressed for a balanced defence policy between East and West, which involved a European willingness to pursue arms modernisation as a means of persuading the Soviet Union to agree to a levelling down of arms capacity; he was instrumental in the establishment of the European Monetary System (EMS) in 1979 to insulate Europe against fluctuations in the value of the American dollar; he pushed forward with the nuclear energy programme following the oil crisis of 1973-4; and, with the aid of his likeminded finance ministers, Hans Apel (1974–8), Hans Matthöfer (1978–82) and Manfred

Lahnstein (1982–3), ensured that a tight, neo-monetarist fiscal policy was pursued, while at the same time being willing to countenance small doses of reflation when essential. Helmut Schmidt thus developed the reputation for being a capable and sensible economic manager, the nation's 'managing director', and he succeeded in increasing West Germany's influence abroad, playing a prominent role within the European Community and at the newly instituted World Economic Summits.

It was, however, the terrorist crisis of 1977 which, in particular, boosted the national standing of Schmidt, gaining him the nickname of the 'Iron Chancellor'. First, on 5 September 1977, Hann-Martin Schleyer, the leader of the German Employers Association (BDA), was kidnapped by the Red Army Faction who demanded the release of eleven jailed terrorists, including their imprisoned former leader Andreas Baader. Then, on 13 October, a Lufthansa airliner, en route between Majorca and Frankfurt and with 86 passengers on board, was hijacked by PLO and German terrorists who called upon the West German government to meet the demands of the Red Army Faction. Two years earlier, in February 1975, the Schmidt government had given in and released five terrorists following the kidnapping of the CDU party leader in West Berlin, Peter Lorenz. The released terrorists subsequently returned to West Germany and committed further acts of murder. Chancellor Schmidt thus determined in 1977 not to concede to the terrorists' demands and instead sought a covert military solution. On the evening of 17 October a crack squad of German anti-terrorist troops boarded the Lufthansa airliner at Mogadishu (in Somalia), stunned the hi-jackers and successfully freed the hostages. Hans-Martin Schleyer was murdered in retaliation on the next day in Mulhouse, but Schmidt's actions succeeded in breaking the back of the terrorist menace (see pages 79-82) — precipitating the suicide of three prominent terrorist leaders held at Stammheim jail, including Andreas Baader. Schmidt's strategy at Mogadishu had been high-risk — the Chancellor later stated that if the scheme had failed he would have tendered his resignation to the Bundestag on 18 October — but, with its success, the Chancellor, termed the 'Hero of Mogadishu', enjoyed a wave of unprecedented popularity which was to remain throughout his period in office.

## 1980-82: The Closing Years Of The Schimdt Era
### The October 1980 federal election

Strains were beginning to grow within the SPD and between the

SPD and FDP coalition partners on economic and defence issues during the closing years of the 1970s. However, Chancellor Schmidt, aided by the firm support of the SPD and FDP floor leaders, Herbet Wehner and Wolfgang Mischnick, managed to retain unity and push through a series of controversial policies — a tough new anti-terrorism law, adherence to the November 1979 decision by NATO to deploy medium-range American nuclear missiles in Europe from 1983, and the expansion of West Germany's nuclear energy programme. Chancellor Schmidt and his economics and finance ministers continued to pursue a tight monetary policy, keeping inflation under firm control, before agreeing to some pump-priming after the Bonn 'Western Summit' in July 1978 to produce a mild pre-election boom and a dent in the unemployment total. The 61-year-old Helmut Schmidt thus contested the October 1980 Bundestag election as a popular statesmanlike figure with a reputation for decision, judgement and integrity. He was opposed by the 65-year-old Franz-Josef Strauss, a flamboyant and radical regionalist leader, revered in Bavaria, but feared elsewhere — particularly in the liberal and predominantly Protestant north.

The public divisions within the CDU-CSU and the machinations of Strauss between 1976 and 1979 reflected unfavourably on the opposition party grouping during the run up to the October 1980 Bundestag election. During the six preceding state elections the CDU lost support and the SPD gained ground — increasing their vote by more than 3% in Rhineland-Palatinate (March 1979), Saarland (April 1980) and North-Rhine-Westphalia (May 1980). The SPD-FDP victory in the October 1978 Hesse election was of particular importance — defeat here would have given the CDU-CSU a two-thirds majority in the Bundersrat and thus an effective veto over all future federal legislation in the absence of a similar countervailing SPD-FDP two-thirds majority in the Bundestag.

The 'Strauss factor' operated against the CDU-CSU alliance in October 1980, with opinion polls registering a 2: 1 popular preference for Schmidt over Strauss and with one in seven of supporters of the CDU favouring Schmidt rather than Strauss as the nation's future Chancellor. The election campaign itself was dull, reworking the old issues of Ostpolitik and political extremism. Helmut Schmidt, with the Soviet invasion of Afghanistan in December 1979, the Iran-Iraq Gulf war and contemporary unrest in Poland capturing public attention, made foreign policy the central electoral issue. He visited Moscow in the summer of 1980 and, utilising the campaign slogan 'Security for the Eighties', projected

27

himself as a responsible statesman seeking to maintain cordial international relations in a deteriorating global situation. He stressed the value of detente and Ostpolitik in reducing East-West tensions and denounced the Russophobe Strauss as a threat to peace and as too unpredictable to be entrusted with control over West Germany's foreign affairs. It was indeed over the issue of Strauss himself that the typically lengthy and personalised German election campaign ignited — left wing groups, who branded Strauss a 'neo-fascist', violently disrupted his public meetings; while Catholic bishops controversially circulated a pastoral letter to their congregations on 21 September which pledged support for Strauss and warned against the dangers of an escalation in public debt if the SPD-FDP coalition was re-elected.

Strauss attempted to moderate his foreign policy stance and subdue his dramatic oratory in an effort to soften his popular image. In addition, he gathered together a balanced shadow-cabinet team which included representatives from all the regional and ideo-logical wings of the CDU and CSU — although Helmut Kohl remained excluded. In the end, however, Strauss's forceful person-ality, his defence posture, his free-market, anti-union economic strategy and his close relationship with Catholic and Bavarian nationalism scared off key sections of the electorate from voting for the CDU — particularly blue-collar workers and northern Pro-testants. Thus the CDU-CSU suffered a humbling and significant defeat on 5 October 1980, its share of the federal vote falling by 4.1% to only 44.5%, which enabled the SPD-FDP coalition to restore its Bundestag majority to 45 seats (see Table 6). In Lower Saxony and Schleswig-Holstein in the north, the CDU vote fell even further, by 5.9% and 5.2% respectively (see Table 7). The CDU-CSU alliance still remained, however, the largest single party in the Bundestag after the October 1980 election — the improvements in its organisation prevented a more crushing defeat.

The SPD's share of the federal vote remained almost constant at 42.9%, displaying a wide divergence between the personal popularity of the Chancellor — who enjoyed a national 'approval rating' of more than 70% — and that of his party and giving further evidence of the stagnation in SPD support which had been apparent since the mid-1970s. It was the liberal FDP who benefited most from the Strauss and Schmidt 'factors'.

The FDP had for long been the recipient of the disgruntled 'floating voter' who opposed extremism in either of the two major parties, particularly at federal elections. The party had also attracted

**Table 6 The October 1980 Bundestag Election**
**(Turnout 87.8%)[1]**

|  | ('000) Zweitstimmen Votes | (%) Share of Total Vote | Seats |
|---|---|---|---|
| SPD | 16 262 | 42.9 | 218*[2] |
| CDU | 12 992 | 34.2 | 174 |
| CSU | 3 908 | 10.3 | 52 |
| FDP | 4 031 | 10.6[3] | 53 |
| GREENS | 568 | 1.5 | 0 |
| DKP | 72 | 0.2 | 0 |
| NPD | 68 | 0.2 | 0 |
| OTHERS | 41 | 0.1 | 0 |
| TOTAL | 37 942 | 100.0 | 497[4] |

[1] Excluding West Berlin
[2] This includes one 'overhang' seat in Schleswig-Holstein
[3] The FDP gained only 7.2% of constituency (Erststimmen) votes
[4] 120 of CDU-CSU and 128 of SPD seats were Erststimmen, won directly at the constituency level. All the FDP's seats, as usual, were Zweitstimmen 'list' seats.

**Table 7 Länder Distribution of Bundestag (Zweitstimmen) Votes in 1980**

|  | SPD | | CDU* | | FDP | |
|---|---|---|---|---|---|---|
|  | 1980 | (1976) | 1980 | (1976) | 1980 | (1976) |
| Bremen | 52.5% | (54.0%) | 28.7% | (32.5%) | 15.0% | (11.8%) |
| Hamburg | 51.7% | (52.6%) | 31.2% | (35.8%) | 14.1% | (10.2%) |
| N. Rhine-Westphalia | 46.8% | (46.9%) | 40.6% | (44.5%) | 10.9% | (7.8%) |
| Schleswig-Holstein | 46.7% | (46.4%) | 38.9% | (44.1%) | 12.7% | (8.8%) |
| Saarland | 48.3% | (46.1%) | 42.3% | (46.2%) | 7.8% | (6.6%) |
| Lower Saxony | 46.9% | (45.7%) | 39.8% | (45.7%) | 11.3% | (7.9%) |
| Hesse | 46.4% | (45.7%) | 40.6% | (44.8%) | 10.6% | (8.5%) |
| Rhineland-Palatinate | 42.8% | (41.7%) | 45.6% | (49.9%) | 9.8% | (7.6%) |
| Baden-Württemberg | 37.2% | (36.6%) | 48.5% | (53.3%) | 12.0% | (9.1%) |
| Bavaria | 32.7% | (32.8%) | 57.6% | (60.0%) | 7.8% | (6.2%) |
| National Average | 42.9% | (42.6%) | 44.5% | (48.6%) | 10.6% | (7.9%) |

* CSU in Bavaria

## Table 8 Party Support by Social Categories in October 1980

| | CDU—CSU % | SPD % | FDP % | % of Population in such a Category |
|---|---|---|---|---|
| 18-24 Year Olds | 9 | 12 | 12 | 11 |
| 25-29 Year Olds | 7 | 10 | 4 | 9 |
| 30-59 Year Olds | 54 | 56 | 63 | 55 |
| Over 60s | 30 | 23 | 22 | 16 |
| Men | 46 | 46 | 43 | 45 |
| Women | 54 | 54 | 57 | 55 |
| Towns of less than 5000 | 22 | 11 | 17 | 16 |
| Cities of over 100 000 | 31 | 41 | 48 | 37 |
| Trade Unionists | 23 | 41 | 24 | 32 |
| Catholics | 59 | 38 | 43 | 46 |
| Protestants | 39 | 55 | 50 | 48 |
| Regular Churchgoers | 36 | 9 | 20 | 20 |
| Unskilled Workers | 11 | 11 | 5 | 11 |
| Skilled Workers | 23 | 33 | 18 | 27 |
| Salaried Workers | 34 | 37 | 37 | 35 |
| Managers/Officials | 7 | 6 | 10 | 7 |
| Professional/Self Employed | 15 | 7 | 19 | 11 |
| Farmers/Landowners | 4 | — | 4 | 2 |

in new groups of white collar voters, business executives and managers during the 1970s as it adopted a more attractive and reformist policy stance of 'social liberalism'. However, its performance in Länder elections between 1976 and 1980 had been most erratic — falling below 5% in Hamburg and Lower Saxony in June 1978, holding on at 6% in Bavaria and Hesse in October 1978, improving on its previous poll in Rhineland-Palatinate and West Berlin in March 1979, before then falling below 5% again at North Rhine-Westphalia in May 1980. During these Länder elections the FDP vote had been squeezed by the new force of the environmentalist Greens. However, in the October 1980 federal election voting became more polarised and the FDP once again gained the support of many moderate minded 'floating voters', particularly former CDU voters frightened by the candidature of Franz-Josef Strauss. To these voters were added the split tactical 'list votes' cast by right-of-centre SPD supporters who, following Helmut Schmidt's injunctions, voted to maintain a steadying influence over the future government. With this diverse base of new support, the FDP's share of the federal vote rose from 7.9% to 10.6% — its highest level since 1961 — and its Bundestag seat representation increased from 39 to 53. (See Table 6).

## The significance of 1980?

(a) The Discredited Radical Option — The candidature of the controversial Franz-Josef Strauss has obscured interpretations of the 1980 federal election result. It remains debatable whether, with the popularity enjoyed by Chancellor Schmidt and the temporary economic recovery he had engineered, a different CDU leader could have made a substantial enough breakthrough to gain a governing majority. Indeed only once in its history, in 1957, had the CDU gained more than 50% of the national vote and no ruling government had been voted out of office in the Fourth Reich — the 1966 and 1969 changes in administrations resulting instead from shifts in the alignment of coalitions. What is clear, however, is that the SPD-FDP era was nearing its close between 1976 and 1980, with the CDU-CSU's internecine disputes during this period and the candidature of Strauss serving merely to prolong its life for a further two years. Secondly, Strauss's stand for the Chancellorship and his subsequent failure discredited at last the much vaunted radical-conservative route to power and forced the party to return to the middle course set out in 1976 by Helmut Kohl. The authority of Strauss was significantly diminished, while that of Kohl, who had acted with propriety and loyalty during the upheavals of 1979-80, was considerably strengthened. The days of a rapprochement between the CDU and FDP were thus paradoxically brought closer by the failed candidature of Strauss.

(b) The Re-Emergence of Minor Parties — While the verdict of the 1980 Bundestag election was equivocal for West Germany's two principal parties, it was much clearer in signalling a revival among the minor parties. The improvement in FDP fortunes was only one example of this revival. An even more significant development was the rise to prominence of the amorphous new environmentalist group, the Green Party. Such a re-emergence of smaller parties was brought about by the uncertainty surrounding West German politics as the country prepared for another *Machtwechsel* and also by the growing popular antipathy towards the larger parties, which had become remote and tainted by corruption scandals, and by a mounting desire for more effective participation in a new style of politics.

The earliest indications of this new public mood were the multitude of 'Citizens' Initiatives Groups' (*Bürgerinitiativen*) which sprang up in West Germany during the early 1970s, campaigning locally for nurseries and children's playgrounds and protesting against environmental pollution and transport policies. They represented an advance upon the more self-centred, 'opting-out' (*Ohne-mich Bewegung*) student protest groups of the mid-1960s and they involved young, educated white-collar and professional groups (particularly teachers), who were concerned above all with the quality of life rather than with material consumerism. By 1973 two million West Germans were involved with such 'citizen lobbies', a number which exceeded the total membership of the major political parties (1.8 million). Such organisations proved attractive, in addition, for the style of politics which they offered, a style which was more direct and participatory than that of the increasingly distant and bureaucratic 'systems parties'. This growing interest in both political issues and direct participation, which was reflected in the opinion polls and electoral campaigns of the later 1970s, contrasted starkly with the German people's deliberate withdrawal from political debate during the 1950s.

These citizen groups remained, however, intensely localised, transient and narrowly-focused bodies during the early 1970s. It was the 1973−4 energy crisis which triggered off a wider movement basing itself around the environment issue. The energy crisis (see pp 89-92 brought into focus West Germany's critical dependence upon imported energy and the future limits to economic growth. Chancellor Schmidt reacted by sanctioning a major expansion in Germany's nuclear power programme utilising the fast breeder reactor. This encouraged, first, the formation of a series of regionally based action groups in Baden-Württemberg and Schleswig-Holstein between 1974-6 to protest against planned new power stations at Wyhl and Brokdorf respectively. Then, in 1977, local environmentalist groups decided to band together in a national coalition termed the Federal League of Citizen Groups for the Protection of the Environment, from which body the Green Party (*Die Grünen*) was to emerge in January 1980. This group, termed the 'Green Alternative Lists' (GAL), contested the Hamburg and Lower Saxony Länder elections in June 1978, gaining 4.5% and 3.9% of the vote respectively (18% in one Lower Saxony constituency — Gorleben — where a nuclear fuel reprocessing plant was planned), and they won 3.2% of the federal vote in the June 1979 contest for the European Parliament. They made an even more significant breakthrough in the October 1979 Bremen city-state and March 1980 Baden-Württemberg Länder contests, when they exceeded the 5% limit and gained their first seats in state parliaments.

The performance of the Greens in the October 1980 Bundestag

election was disappointing, the party only mustering 1.5% of the national vote after its vote had been squeezed during a polarised campaign. The party also suffered during this election from the emergence in public of stark divisions within its ranks between conservative, agrarian ecologists and ultra-leftist radicals. The latter grouping, which included a number of former communists, gained ascendancy in the party during 1980 and forced through a strongly left-wing, anti-NATO and anti-growth, manifesto programme. This led to a large number of resignations of conservative members, including the popular author and former CDU Bundestag deputy, Herbert Gruhl (who was the founder and leader of the autonomous *Grüne Aktion Zukunft* — GAZ) and the Greens' centrist chairman, August Haussleiter, who stepped down at the June 1980 Dortmund pre-election conference to be replaced by Dieter Burgmann.[1] The party recovered from this split and temporary setback, however, and gained significantly in strength between 1980 and 1983. During these years the party's organisation improved and the issues for which it campaigned — defence and the environment — moved to the centre of the national stage as the SPD-FDP government pressed, following the 1979—80 oil price hike, for energy conservation and as a broad debate opened up within the NATO countries over the proposed stationing of new medium-range nuclear missiles. The Greens during this period became increasingly radical. They established new campaigns for the introduction of lead-free petrol and emission controls to check acid rain and pressed for a halting of the nuclear energy programme. In the sphere of defence, the party developed a distinctive unilateralist programme which opposed the deployment of Cruise and Pershing-II missiles in Western Europe, which called for the disbandment of NATO and the Warsaw Pact, which opposed enlistment in the Bundeswehr (territorial army), and which sought the creation of a neutral demilitarised zone throughout Europe. The party's economic programme also continued its leftward lurch, which had first become apparent at the March 1980 Saarbrücken conference when the party's rank and file had voted for greater state control over large corporations, the introduction of a 35-hour working week and the unlimited right to strike. This led to fears that the Greens were turning red.

The Greens remained, however, an amorphous body, drawing

---

[1] These conservative ecologists formed a new, but unsuccessful, grouping, the Ecological Democratic Party in 1981.

together a wide amalgam of diverse groups — pacifists, alternatives, feminists, environmentalists, squatters and the young unemployed — including disenchanted former supporters of the ruling coalition. After the federal poll of October 1980, the party made further advances in Länder elections — gaining representation in West Berlin (May 1981 — 7.2%), Lower Saxony (June 1982 — 6.5%). Hamburg (June 1982 — 7.7%: December 1982 — 6.8%) and Hesse (September 1982 — 8%) — and in council elections, holding over 1000 council seats by March 1982. In addition, the Greens organised huge demonstrations in cities and at military sites in opposition to the installation of nuclear missiles — one such demonstration at Bonn on 10 October 1981 was attended by 300 000 people — and the construction of nuclear power stations — 100 000 protestors gathering at Hanover in Lower Saxony to demonstrate against the Gorleben reprocessing project in March 1979 and 80 000 people marching on Brokdorf in Schleswig-Holstein in February 1981.

The rise of the Greens was facilitated by the German electoral system. Proportional representation gave the Greens seats in local areas where it was able to muster support from radical rural and white-collar groups — Baden-Württemberg, the 'cradle of the ecological movement', was a classic example.[1] This created a publicity platform for further successes. In addition, the 1967 Party Law (*Parteiengesetz*) granted state finance (to help reimburse campaign expenses) to parties receiving more than 0.5% of the federal vote — this brought in DM 2 million to the Greens following the 1980 election.[2] The Greens themselves added a new dimension to West German politics by questioning many of the assumptions of the existing system. They proved unwilling at first to enter into coalitions at the Länder level, often asking intolerable prices for their support; they campaigned strongly for local issues — opposing, for example, the construction of an additional runway at Frankfurt airport or extensions to Hamburg port; and they pressed for a new form of rank-and-file, anti-personality politics — establishing a collective executive leadership, alternating their elected *Landtage* delegates every two years and opposing increases

[1] In Baden-Württemberg the Greens in addition benefited from the traditional rivalry and enmity between the population of Baden who resisted dominance by the Swabians of Württemberg.

[2] The Party Law, which operates at both the federal and state level, reimburses parties for a proportion of their election expenses on a scale (see page 51) determined by the number of votes achieved.

in deputies' salaries. This was a challenge to the main parties and affected, in particular, the left-of-centre SPD and FDP. Support was drawn away from these two parties during the years between 1980 and 1983, with adverse electoral consequences. For the SPD the challenge of the Greens exacerbated internal tensions already evident between its right and left wings, before accommodation was later attempted on a green-tinged programme.

## 1981-82: The Disintegration of the SPD-FDP Coalition

Despite gaining an impressive electoral victory in October 1980, cracks rapidly appeared in the eleven year SPD-FDP coalition during the spring of 1981. Economic and defence policies remained the critical issues. The SPD had always possessed a radical urban and university educated 'youth' wing (the *Jungsocialisten* or *Jusos,* which was open to members under the age of 35), many of whom looked back upon Bad Godesberg as a betrayal of the party's Marxist principles, others of whom looked forward to a new form of participatory and decentralised socialism. This wing, which included many who had been radicalised as supporters of the APO student movement in 1968 before later joining the SPD, moved higher up within the party's ranks during the early 1980s and became increasingly alienated from the leadership of the moderate and pragmatic Helmut Schmidt — some leaving Bonn to construct a new and more radical form of socialism at the Länder level (particularly in Hamburg, Hesse, the Saarland, Schleswig-Holstein and Baden-Württemberg). The SPD's radical wing, like the Greens, favoured unilateralism, opposed nuclear power and were ambivalent to West Germany's continued membership of NATO. In addition, they favoured greater state control over the economy, including a thoroughgoing programme of nationalisation. The strength of the SPD's left wing within the Bundestag — a grouping which was termed the Leverkusen Circle (after the Ruhr town where they first met) — increased from around 30 to over 50 deputies (out of 218) following the October 1980 federal election. At the SPD's June 1980 pre-election conference at Essen, they accounted for a similar proportion, around 20%, of the conference delegates, forcing fudged compromises over nuclear issues.

These internal divisions were temporarily masked by the 1978-80 economic recovery and by the need to close ranks for the October 1980 federal election. However, with the sudden downturn in the West German economy between 1980 and 1982 a wide cleavage

35

opened within the party. The economic indicators began to move sharply against the government during the winter of 1980, as both prices and unemployment raced upwards. By December 1981 unemployment had reached 1.7 million and by the winter of 1982 the figure exceeded two million. Chancellor Schmidt responded to this deteriorating situation by introducing tight deflationary budgets in the autumns of 1980 and 1981 in which state borrowing was pegged back, with childrens' allowances and public sector wages being reduced, while defence spending (in accordance with 1979 NATO pledges) was allowed to increase in real terms. The Chancellor was driven on in this direction by his FDP coalition colleagues, who, following their electoral success in October 1980, sought to exert an even greater influence over federal policy and who now favoured a shift away from Keynesianism towards freer-market liberalism. Schmidt himself, however, also believed in the need to maintain firm control over welfare spending programmes and to keep in check public spending as a proportion of GNP so as not to overburden and choke off the wealth creating industrial sector through mounting tax liabilities. This led to jibes by SPD leftwingers that Schmidt was the 'best CDU Chancellor we have ever had'. The rightward shift in SPD economic policies persuaded some on the left that a coalition split and a period in opposition might be preferable to continuation in government and that it would enable the party to regenerate with a more socialist policy programme. Conflicts with Chancellor Schmidt, who was now being seen as a traitor to party principles, over defence and environmental issues added weight to this view.

During 1981, support for the SPD rapidly dwindled as the party took the blame for the contemporary recession and as its internal divisions widened. By October 1981, although Helmut Schmidt remained the most popular politician in the country, the opinion poll rating of his party had slumped to barely 33% — its lowest level since the Guillaume spy scandal of April-May 1974. Eight months earlier, in February 1981, the SPD's deputy chairman, Hans-Jürgen Wischnewski, declared that the party was in a worse shape than at any time since 1945. In Schmidt's native city-state of Hamburg, the SPD's leftist mayor, Hans-Ulrich Klose, refused to co-operate over the Brokdorf nuclear power station project, resigning in June 1981, while in the Bundestag, on 27 January 1981, twenty-four SPD rebels, led by Manfred Coppik and Karl-Heinz Hansen, broke the traditional strict discipline of West Germany's parliamentary Fraktionen by voting against increases in the defence budget and arms sales to Saudi Arabia.[1] This was followed in May 1981 by a stunning defeat in the Land election in West Berlin, a city which the SPD-FDP coalition had held almost continuously since 1949 and where the SPD's vote fell to only 38.4%. Recent city government corruption scandals, housing shortages and social unrest contributed to this result, but West Berlin, the flashpoint for Ostpolitik and detente, was viewed as a barometer of the nation and the May 1981 result was taken as an indication that the public had lost faith in the ruling coalition. This interpretation was supported by the collapse of the party's vote in the March 1982 elections in Lower Saxony. Matters were compounded for Chancellor Schmidt during this period by a deterioration in his own personal health — a pacemaker being fitted to his heart in October 1981 — and by major changes within the Chancellery team which deprived him of the advice of Wischnewski, Bölling and Schuler.

During the spring of 1982 there was a temporary upturn in the fortunes of the SPD. The party's Munich conference in April 1982 agreed once more, following a resignation threat by Schmidt, to delay and fudge the issue of acceptance of Cruise and Pershing – II missiles until the close of the US-USSR Geneva arms control talks, while in February 1982 a major new DM 12.5 billion jobs creation programme, which was to be funded by increases in VAT and wealth taxes, was passed by the Bundestag following the Chancellor's successful and unprecedented call of a vote of confidence in his administration. This was followed by a major cabinet re-shuffle on 27 April 1982 — which involved the induction of Manfred Lahnstein (44) as minister of finance, Heinz Westphal (57) as labour and social affairs minister and Frau Anke Fuchs (44) as youth, family and health minister; and the return of Hans-Jürgen Wischnewski as minister of state in the Chancellery and Klaus Bölling as chief government spokesman — aimed at giving new impetus to the ruling coalition. Unfortunately for the Chancellor, however, the administration's rebirth proved to be short-lived, with his FDP coalition colleagues refusing during the summer of 1982 to sanction tax increases to pay for the SPD's proposed public investment programme. The divisions between the coalition partners widened

---

[1] Coppik and Hansen were subsequently excluded from the SPD's Bundestag Fraktion by the party's disciplinary committee in July 1981 and January 1982 respectively and became independents. This prompted the two rebels, following a public meeting attended by 1200 at Recklinghausen (North-Rhine-Westphalia), to form a new leftwing party called the Democratic Socialist Forum (*Forum Demokratische Socialisten*).

and the popularity of the SPD dipped once more. At the June 1982 Hamburg city-state election the SPD's share of the vote slumped by 9% to 42.8%, leaving the CDU as the major party, but the SPD as a minority government dependent upon unpredictable support from the Greens. With the Hesse state elections forthcoming in November Helmut Schmidt was faced with the almost certain probability that the CDU-CSU would at last achieve a two-thirds majority in the Bundesrat and a majority on the Bundestag-Bundesrat Joint Conciliation Committee and would thus be in a position to block his federal programmes.[1]

The FDP was similarly adversely affected by the declining popularity of the Schmidt government. Its vote fell significantly in West Berlin in May 1981 and in the Lower Saxony and Hamburg contests of March and June 1982, it dropped sharply below the earlier federal election level. During the years between 1969−80 the FDP had been in full accordance with the SPD on foreign policy and Ostpolitik and on domestic human rights issues. They had, however, as free-market liberals by inclination, only been luke-warm supporters of the SPD's economic policies. From the summer of 1981 the FDP leader, Hans-Dietrich Genscher, concerned with the party's electoral future, began to talk openly about an approaching *Wende* (turning point) and secret negotiations commenced between the FDP and CDU at the Land and federal level. The FDP had temporarily joined with the CDU as coalition partners in Lower Saxony between 1976−8 and had continued to operate with the CDU in the Saarland since 1977, where they came to the unique agreement that the state's three votes in the Bundersrat would not be employed in a manner which would harm the federal SPD-FDP coalition. In February 1981 a number of FDP delegates temporarily rebelled against the party leadership in West Berlin and precipitated the resignation of the SPD mayor Dietrich Stobbe. It was, however, the decision of the FDP Land party conference in Hesse on 17 June 1982 to form a coalition pact with the CDU for the forthcoming elections in September, which, when ratified by the federal FDP's national presidium by a 15-3 margin, was the first clear indication that a full split with the SPD was imminent.

The CDU had, meanwhile, been quietly rebuilding under the leadership of Helmut Kohl after the turmoil of 1979−80. They

[1] In June 1982 the CDU (including its 3 votes from Saarland) had a 26-15 majority in the Bundesrat. A victory in Hesse would have tipped the balance over required 28, to 30-11.

performed well in the Lower Saxony and Hamburg polls of mid-1982, and in the West Berlin election of May 1981 they finally captured control (with the 'toleration' of the FDP), following years of patient nursing by their popular leader, Richard Von Weizsäcker. The decisive moment for the party came on 9 September 1982, when the FDP's federal economics minister, Count Otto Graf Lambsdorff, presented a memorandum to Chancellor Schmidt calling for major cuts in welfare spending to provide a sound base for economic recovery. This plea for what Schmidt termed the 'elbowing society' conflicted sharply with SPD philosophy and was taken to be a statement of grounds for a divorce which only awaited the final sanction from the forthcoming FDP conference due to be held in November 1982. Chancellor Schmidt decided therefore to act first and he challenged the opposition to attempt to topple the government through employing Article 67 of the Basic Law, the 'constructive vote of no confidence', and, if successful, to seek an early election to gain a full mandate from the people.

## The constitutional crisis of September-October 1982

The 'constructive vote of no confidence' was introduced into the Basic Law in an effort to give greater stability to governments, so as to prevent the formation of the temporary, negative majorities to unseat an incumbent government which had been so common-place in the Weimar period. This constitutional innovation had worked well during the Fourth Reich. Only once, in April 1972, when the CDU-CSU, led by Rainer Barzel, tried to unseat Willy Brandt's precarious coalition, had this procedure been initiated and on that occasion it had been unsuccessful — failing by two votes.

Thus in September 1982 Helmut Kohl, the CDU leader, initially recoiled from taking this risky course and called instead for Chancellor Schmidt to resign. Helmut Schmidt refused and attempted instead to engineer a dissolution through requesting a confidence vote in which the SPD would abstain and the opposition would vote against. This move failed, however, with the opposition, not wishing to leave Schmidt fighting the election as the incumbent Chancellor, refusing to co-operate. It did, nevertheless, persuade the FDP to finally leave the coalition and begin negotiating with the CDU on 17 September 1982. Helmut Schmidt soldiered on for another two weeks at the head of a minority SPD government, taking over the FDP leader's foreign ministry portfolio, before Helmut Kohl called for and won a 'constructive vote of no confidence' motion — polling 256 votes, compared to 235 against and four abstentions. Kohl was sworn in as Chancellor on 1 October 1982 and declared his wish to hold a federal election at an early date.

The employment by the CDU of the 'constructive vote of no confidence' was legitimate under Article 67 of the constitution. The action of the FDP Fraktion was, however, most controversial. In October 1980 they had campaigned with the SPD as part of a four-year coalition pact. This they deserted after barely two years, establishing a new administration with the opposition party. Helmut Schmidt was thus justified when he called in September 1982 for a new Bundestag election to give a genuine mandate to this change in government. The problem, however, for both Schmidt and Kohl, was the lack of provision for midterm elections under the German constitution. Elections outside the four year term were discouraged and had to be engineered by a Chancellor calling for and failing to win, through deliberate abstentions, a vote of confidence (Article 68). This Willy Brandt obtained in September 1972 and Helmut Kohl on 17 December 1982. The Federal President, Karl Carstens (a CDU delegate between 1972–9), although first entertaining reservations concerning the constitutional legality of the move, assented to this orchestrated vote in January 1983, arguing that an early election had been the desire of all four parties and that the formation of a long-term government would have been unlikely without dissolving the Bundestag. This interpretation was supported by the Federal Constitutional Court by a 6:2 margin on 16 February 1983, after the issue had been referred to it by four Bundestag deputies (2 FDP, 1 SPD and 1 CDU). Kohl's tactics remained, nevertheless, controversial. In September 1972 when Chancellor Brandt called for such a vote he had already lost his Bundestag majority through the defection of disaffected deputies. In December 1982, by contrast, Chancellor Kohl possessed a sound and substantial majority. The events of September-December 1982 served to highlight the rigidity of the West German constitution and the controversy which could be provoked by departures from its written principles.

## The March 1983 Federal Election

During the months immediately following the October 1982 Machtwechsel the German public reacted against the machinations in Bonn and became disillusioned in particular with the FDP, which had reneged on its October 1980 electoral pledge and then proceeded to block Helmut Schmidt's call for an immediate fresh election in the winter of 1982. The FDP, with opinion polls recording only 2.3% national support, feared that an early election would result in their annihilation. Some CDU-CSU rightwingers, including Franz-Josef Strauss, looked forward to such a prospect and pressed for an early poll, but Helmut Kohl — anxious to maintain a liberal element within the coalition — agreed upon a delay until March 1983.

This opportunistic delay alienated voters from both the CDU and the FDP in the Länder elections in Hesse (September 1982), Bavaria (October 1982) and Hamburg (December 1982) and provoked a wave of sympathy for Helmut Schmidt and the SPD. It also contributed towards a rise in support for the 'anti-system' party, the Greens. (See the Länder electoral tables in Appendix B). The FDP was reduced in all these contests to between 2.2% and 3.5% of the total vote, with a consequent loss of representation in the Hesse and Bavaria Landtage. The CDU, in turn, failed to wrest Hamburg and Hesse from the SPD and thus did not gain its expected two-thirds majority in the Bundersrat upper chamber.

Sharp internal divisions opened up within the FDP during the months between the September 1982 change of government and the March 1983 Bundestag election. The party, like the SPD, possessed an increasingly vociferous liberal anti-nuclear wing — the Young Democrats (*Jungdemokraten* or *Judos*) — which had been prominent at the June 1981 Cologne conference, when 30% of the delegates opposed the executive's endorsement of NATO's Pershing-II missile deployment decision. This dissent extended within the parliamentary party, with 18 of the FDP's 53 deputies voting for Chancellor Schmidt and two abstaining during the historic 1 October 1982 'confidence vote'. On 4 October 1982, the FDP leadership agreed to an interim coalition programme with the CDU-CSU which included cuts in welfare spending and an enhancement of VAT to finance new investment, and which enabled Hans-Dietrich Genscher, Otto Lambsdorff and Josef Ertl to remain in office as foreign, economics and agriculture ministers. However, radical 'social liberal' deputies, who were firm believers in the party's 1971 progressive Freiburg Theses and who comprised a third of the FDP's Bundestag Fraktion, felt betrayed by this sudden switch in allegiance and made visible their opposition. In October 1982 the interior minister, Gerhart Baum (a former chairman of the Judos), resigned from the government, while the party's general-secretary, Günter Verheugen, went a step further and left the party to join the SPD. Five other FDP deputies abandoned the party in November 1982 — two joining the SPD.

41

This opposition continued at the FDP party conference held in West Berlin on 5-6 November 1982, as old cleavages last visible at the time of the breakaways of 1956 and 1969 re-emerged. This time, however, breakaways occurred on the left. Hans-Dietrich Genscher captured only 57% of the votes cast in the conference's leadership election, his lowest ever total, and, in retaliation, the party's right wing decided to dissolve the rebellious Young Democrat section of the party. This persuaded 1500 defiant radical Free Democrats to hold a conference in Bochum on 27-28 November 1982 at which a new liberal democratic party was suddenly launched. This new body did not establish itself as a credible new political force, but it did increase tensions within the party and serve to persuade further waverers to leave — FDP party membership declining from 86 000 to 80 000 during the last three months of 1982. The FDP thus entered the campaign for the March 1983 Bundestag election as a deeply divided and unpopular party. Its quiet, businesslike leader, Hans-Dietrich Genscher, was an electoral asset in October 1980: in March 1983 he was a liability.

The SPD, by contrast, enjoyed a wave of popular sympathy in the immediate wake of the October 1982 constitutional crisis — the SPD being viewed as the party which had sought to give the electors a voice in the change of federal government, but which had been blocked by the FDP and CDU. However, the SPD was unable to build upon this initial public goodwill, as it failed to decide on a clear sense of direction in the wake of the Machtwechsel. On 26 October 1982 its leader and Chancellor for the previous eight years, the 63-year-old Helmut Schmidt, announced that he would not stand again. This decision was ostensibly taken on the grounds of health. Schmidt was also, however, tired of the internal feuds and back-biting within the SPD and felt unable to work in the future with either the CDU, FDP, or the Greens as a possible coalition partner after the election.

Schmidt was replaced as SPD chancellor-candidate by the 56-year-old Hans-Jöchen Vogel, a former minister of justice and mayor of Munich, who formed a competent, but colourless, substitute.[1]

[1]Vogel, born in Göttingen in February 1926 and educated as a lawyer at Munich University, had been appointed SPD Land chairman in Bavaria in 1972 and elected, in the same year, as mayor of Munich. Between 1975-81 he had served in the Schmidt cabinet as federal justice minister, before being sent to West Berlin to replace Dietrich Stobbe as mayor in January 1981 with the brief to 'clean-up' and overhaul the unpopular local party machine. Vogel was the first Catholic and southern-based leader of the postwar SPD. (His younger brother Bernhard Vogel had been CDU minister-president of Rhineland-Palatinate since 1976).

Power within the party now shifted back towards its idealistic 69-year-old veteran chairman, Willy Brandt. He dreamed of forming a new leftward coalition which would embrace peace campaigners, anti-Genscher Free Democrats, 'alternatives' and Greens, campaigning on a green-tinged programme renouncing Cruise and Pershing-II missiles and nuclear power. Hans-Jöchen Vogel, although drawn from the conservative Kanalarbeiter wing of the party, had sympathy with this 'broad church' view, but did not decisively come out in its favour. The SPD thus entered the March 1983 election in an uncertain mood. Its membership rolls were stagnating and its policy stance remained vague and fudged.

The CDU, by contrast, entered the March 1983 election campaign in a strong, confident and bullish mood. It was beginning to recover from the public's disapproval of its machinations during the autumn of 1982, party membership had increased to over 700 000, and its leader, the 53-year-old Helmut Kohl, had used the months since October 1982 to establish himself as a respected statesman on the domestic and international stage.

The Bundestag election of March 1983 was fought around the dual issues of defence — the imminent installation of Pershing-II missiles — and the economy. The campaign, though lacking the sharp contrast in personalities evident in October 1980, became one of the most ideologically polarised in postwar German history, with the two main parties, the SPD and the CDU, offering policy prescriptions which varied to an unusual degree.

*Defence* — The SPD, while not rejecting the stationing of Pershing-II missiles if absolutely necessary, stressed the 'twin-track' aspects of the November 1979 NATO agreement — the commitment on the part of the United States to enter into serious arms-control talks with the Soviet Union, with Cruise and Pershing-II installation existing only as a final option. Hans-Jöchen Vogel, Willy Brandt, Egon Bahr (the SPD's defence spokesman) and even Helmut Schmidt were not, however, convinced that the American President, Ronald Reagan, had made a genuine effort to reach an arms-control agreement or to respond to Soviet concessions made in January 1983. The SPD thus sought greater an effort on the part of the US and USSR to reach a compromise solution and withheld its final decision on deployment until the outcome of the Geneva arms talks was known. The CDU and FDP, while also hoping for progress at Geneva, were by contrast more willing to give unconditional support to their American allies and to accept deployment in the winter of 1983. They accused the SPD of lacking full commitment to NATO and of being influenced by the Soviet Union, whose foreign minister, Andrei Gromyko, had published an article in *Pravda* (the organ of the Soviet Communist Party) calling for all European countries to resist NATO's re-armament initiative 'as an indication of political maturity'.

*The Economy* — The economic programme presented by the SPD to the West German electorate in March 1983 also differed significantly from that presented by the ruling CDU-FDP coalition. The SPD campaigned for an increase in the level of taxes on high income earners to provide funds for state 'job creation' investment; for a shorter working week; for the extension of workers' participation in industry; and for a reform of the EEC's Common Agricultural Policy, so as to reduce food stockpiles and price levels. The ruling coalition advocated, in contrast, a reduction in the level of the government's budget deficit through the enforcement of economies in the social services and by reducing industrial subsidies; the promotion of private enterprise and investment; a lowering in tax levels; and the continued progress of the nuclear energy programme. Chancellor Kohl campaigned under the optimistic, forward-looking slogan 'Vote for the Upturn' and spoke of a new mood in the country which favoured reduced government interference and a turnaround in broader economic and moral values. His programme was strongly supported by business interest groups who threatened to launch an 'investment strike' if the SPD was elected to power.

The campaign was typically scurrilous, being filled with daily 'scandals' unearthed by an inquisitive and sensationalist West German press, the right-wing, mass circulation *Bild Zeitung* even accusing the SPD leader, Hans-Jöchen Vogel, of having been the 'extended arm of Goebbels' in enforcing loyalty to Hitler when he had served as a Hitler Youth leader during the Second World War. Defence was, however, the key issue in the March 1983 election.[1] The country was deeply divided over this issue, but on balance felt more secure with the CDU-CSU's pro-NATO stance. This, coupled with greater confidence in the party's economic programme and a general desire for change following more than a decade of social democracy, propelled the CDU-CSU towards a landslide victory,

[1] Opinion polls during the campaign showed that 56% of the population regarded unemployment and 32% the deployment of nuclear weapons as the key electoral issues. Defence was, however, the decisive polarising 'hinge issue', with SPD supporters — unlike CDU — being evenly split on their attitude towards deployment of Cruise and Pershing-II.

the allied parties gaining their second largest ever share of the national vote, 48.8%, and gaining two million more votes than in October 1980. (See Table 9). The most notable feature of this victory was the major advance made by the CDU in the moderate and Protestant Länder of northern Germany, as the centrist Kohl, in contrast to Strauss in October 1980, proved appealing to northern electors, who were faced on this occasion by a southern-based SPD leader. This advance gave a more even geographical spread to CDU-CSU support in March 1983, significantly reducing the traditional Main river electoral divide. [1]

The SPD, deprived of the 'Schmidt factor', which polls had suggested had brought the party an extra 5% of support in the previous election[2], and burdened by the disappointing economic record of its final years in power, managed to capture only 38.2% of the national vote — its most disappointing showing since 1961. It retained much of its traditional working class, skilled and unskilled workers, support, but suffered a haemorrhage among middle class and white-collar electors, losing more than a million such votes to both the CDU-CSU and the Greens. It was however, the FDP who, as expected, fared worst, capturing only 6.9% of the national vote and losing a third of its 1980 support (1.3 million votes). The FDP managed nevertheless — with the help of CDU 'ticket-splitting' — to surmount the 5% electoral hurdle and continued to hold (with 34 seats) the balance of power in the Bundestag. However, in the Länder elections in Rhineland-Palatinate and Schleswig-Holstein in March 1983 the FDP vote slumped to 3.5% and 2.2% — below the threshold for Landtag representation. Thus by April 1983 the FDP held seats in only five Länder assemblies — Baden-Württemberg, Bremen, Lower Saxony, Saarland and West Berlin — six years before they had been represented in all Landtage.

The FDP, although still holding the balance at the centre, could only barely maintain its claim to be West Germany's third party after the March 1983 Bundestag election and the contemporary Länder polls. The Greens now closely challenged the FDP, holding seats in five Landtage (Baden-Württemberg, Bremen, West Berlin, Hamburg and Lower Saxony) and capturing 5.6% of the national vote in the federal election. They became the first new party since

[1]In the large state of North-Rhine-Westphalia, for example, the CDU's vote climbed from 40.6% of the total to 45.8%, pushing the SPD into second position.
[2]In March 1983, by contrast, Helmut Kohl, benefiting from the 'Chancellor bonus' that came from incumbency in the Federal Republic, led his SPD challenger, Hans-Jöchen Vogel, by a 44% to 37% approval rating respectively.

45

**Table 9 The March 1983 Bundestag Election**
**(Turnout 89.1%)**

| | ('000) Zweitstimmen Votes | (%) Share of Total Vote | Seats |
|---|---|---|---|
| SPD | 14 866 | 38.2 | 193[1] |
| CDU | 14 857 | 38.2 | 191 |
| CSU | 4 140 | 10.6 | 53 |
| FDP | 2 706 | 6.9[2] | 34 |
| GREENS | 2 165 | 5.6 | 27 |
| DKP | 66 | 0.2 | 0 |
| NPD | 91 | 0.2 | 0 |
| OTHERS | 47 | 0.1 | 0 |
| TOTAL | 39 280 | 100.0 | 498[3] |

[1] These include two 'overhang seats' in Bremen and Hamburg.
[2] These FD- gained only 2.8% of Erststimmen votes.
[3] The CDU-CSU captured 180 direct Ertstimmen constituency seats, the SPD 68.

1957 to gain seats in the Bundestag and to break the monopoly of the three 'system parties'. With defence being such a prominent issue in the March 1983 election campaign, the Greens had been able to break out of their threatened regional ghetto and gain recognition as a national party, drawing votes away from both the SPD and FDP and capturing 23% of the votes cast by young first-time electors. At one stage during the campaign, with support for the Greens exceeding 6% and with the FDP promising to fall below the 5% threshold, the possibility briefly emerged of the Greens holding the balance of power. The 'Green vote' was, however, squeezed during the closing weeks of the campaign and the FDP was saved. The Greens had nevertheless arrived on the federal stage. It remained to be seen, however, whether the party's presence would be permanent and whether the Greens would develop from being a single issue 'peace party' into a more broadly-based and challenging new force in West German politics.

## West German Politics Under Helmut Kohl: 1983-87

### The CDU-CSU-FDP coalition in power

Helmut Kohl was relieved that the FDP had managed to surmount the 5% electoral hurdle and continued to hold the balance of power in the Bundestag after March 1983. They provided for Chancellor

Kohl, as for his predecessor Helmut Schmidt, a useful counter-weight to the governing party's more extreme wing — in this case Franz-Josef Strauss's CSU — enabling Kohl to pursue a centre-right policy programme.

Helmut Kohl assembled a cabinet of seventeen which included three members of the FDP — holding three of the six 'classic ministries' (foreign, defence, economics, finance, interior and justice) — and five members of the CSU. (See Table 10). The FDP lost the interior ministry to the CSU rightwinger Friedrich Zimmermann in the October 1982 transfer of power (gaining the justice ministry in compensation). They were now also, as a result of the contraction in their parliamentary strength, deprived of the agricultural ministry, which had been held by the controversial pro-farmer Bavarian, Josef Ertl (58), since 1969. The FDP still, however, retained a strong voice in the decision-making process. The CSU captured the important interior (home office) ministry and the agricultural and transport portfolios — enabling the party to uphold the interests of the small farmers and car and aircraft industries of Bavaria. However, the party's ambitious leader, Franz-Josef Strauss, who had openly sought the office of foreign secretary (held since 1974 by the FDP leader Hans-Dietrich Genscher) and had turned down the offer of a minor ministry, remained outside Bonn, continuing as minister-premier of Bavaria. Strauss was to criticise the Kohl administration from the wings, obstruct its policies through his influential position in the Bundesrat, and embarrass the government with his frequent overseas visits as an unofficial and self-appointed foreign minister.

Chancellor Kohl's cabinet contained a mixture of moderates (including Stoltenberg and Geissler) and conservatives and, although promising during the election campaign a significant turn towards the right, the policy programme of his new government did not differ markedly from that pursued by Helmut Schmidt. Ostpolitik remained in place under the continued direction of Hans-Dietrich Genscher (56) — although the new administration remained more firmly committed to the US relationship and to the November 1979 NATO arms modernisation programme. In economic affairs, change was gradual and progressive, with strong emphasis now being given towards reducing the budget deficit (through welfare economies) and, later on, towards 'new conservative' liberalisation, de-regulation and privatisation. The most sudden and significant change was at the interior ministry, where, with Friedrich Zimmermann replacing the 'social liberal' Gerhart

Baum, policy shifted sharply to the right and sanction was now given to the introduction of computerised identity cards, stricter immigration controls and a tough new law on demonstrations. There were, secondly, major changes at the top of West Germany's politicised federal civil service — as had previously occurred immediately following the 1969 Machtwechsel — among the ranks of the *Beamten* under-secretaries and the ministerial directors (*Staatssekretäre*). Chancellor Kohl, in addition, brought into the Chancellery his own team of personal advisers and secretaries — these included his foreign-policy adviser Horst Teltschik, his chief-of-staff Waldemar Schreckenberger (an old school friend), his communications director Eduard Ackermann, his loyal secretary Frau Juliane Weber, and Philipp Jenninger (who handled relations with East Germany).

**Table 10 The Kohl Administration Cabinet of March 1987**

| | | |
|---|---|---|
| Dr Helmut Kohl | CDU | Federal Chancellor |
| Hans-Dietrich Genscher | FDP | Vice-Chancellor & Foreign Affairs |
| Dr Manfred Wörner | CDU | Defence |
| Dr Otto Graf Lambsdorff | FDP | Economic Affairs |
| Dr Gerhard Stoltenberg | CDU | Finance |
| Dr Friedrich Zimmermann | CSU | Interior |
| Hans Engelhard | FDP | Justice |
| Ignaz Kiechle | CSU | Agriculture |
| Dr Werner Dollinger | CSU | Transport |
| Norbert Blüm | CDU | Labour & Social Affairs |
| Frau-Dr Dorothee Wilms | CDU | Education |
| Heiner Geissler | CDU | Youth, Family & Health Affairs |
| Dr Oscar Schneider | CSU | Housing Construction |
| Heinrich Windelen | CDU | Inter-German Affairs |
| Dr Jürgen Warnke | CSU | Economic Co-operation |
| Dr Christian Schwarz-Schilling | CDU | Posts & Telecommunications |
| Dr Heinz Riesenhuber | CDU | Research & Technology |

Despite this pool of personal advisers, Helmut Kohl rapidly developed the reputation of being a detached and cautious Chancellor, in contrast to the sharp-minded and decisive Helmut Schmidt who had taken a keen personal interest in economic management, foreign affairs and a number of other policy pro-grammes, for example the nuclear energy programme. Helmut Kohl, by contrast, took a more detached view of his office. He presided over the cabinet in a manner akin to that of a chairman of a board of directors, delegating great authority to his ministers, who were allowed to get on with their jobs, while being assured that they could rely on the loyal support of the Chancellor during periods of personal crisis. Such crises afflicted the Kohl administration with an unusual frequency during the first three years of its life, as first the Kiessling and then the Flick and Tiedge scandals rocked the government and led to the resignations of key cabinet ministers.

One factor which explained this change in Chancellorship style was the personality and natural inclinations of Kohl himself. The new Chancellor, who had gradually worked his way up the CDU state ladder in Rhineland-Palatinate during the 1960s[1] before being elected federal party chairman in 1973, was by temperament more of a party politician than an administrator or strategic thinker. As Chancellor, therefore, he was to devote far more time to the crucial, but often mundane, affairs of backroom and town-hall party politics, building up alliances and firm support bases for himself and his legislative programme across the Länder, than his predecessor Helmut Schmidt, who delegated such activities to his party lieutenants, Willy Brandt and Herbert Wehner, and concentrated instead on administrative problem-solving and international statesmanship. The second crucial factor, however, was the unusually diverse and unstable nature of the new CDU-CSU-FDP governing coalition. Chancellor Kohl had to seek to maintain a working relationship with two troublesome coalition partners — one, the FDP, which found itself being torn apart by scandals and divisions: the other, the CSU, led by the unpredictable Franz-Josef Strauss. A series of periodic co-ordinating meetings were arranged in order to attempt to quietly settle such intra-coalition differences behind closed doors and to co-ordinate broad policy strategies. Much, however, was left to the discretion of individual ministers.

During 1983, despite the continuing economic recession (with unemployment now exceeding two million), Chancellor Kohl and the CDU-CSU-FDP coalition continued to profit from the defence issue. 1983 was the 'year of the missiles', distinguished by a rising tide of popular protest which culminated in huge demonstrations in Bonn, Hamburg and Stuttgart on 22 October as the anti-nuclear

---

[1] Helmut Kohl, born in April 1930 into a Roman Catholic family based in Ludwigshafen (Rhineland-Palatinate), studied law and history at Frankfurt and Heidelberg Universities and worked initially in the chemical industry. In 1959 he was elected to the Rhineland-Palatinate Landtag, rising to become state minister-president in 1969.

49

lobby sought to prevent the stationing of Pershing-II missiles.[1] The Pershing-II issue seriously divided the opposition SPD, who finally came out against deployment at their November 1983 conference. The CDU-CSU-FDP coalition, by contrast, adopted a consistent line in support of the United States and deployment, which remained the majority view in the country. By November 1983, with the Pershing-II deployment vote in the Bundestag won, Chancellor Kohl (dubbed the 'Rocket Chancellor' by opposition leader Hans-Jöchen Vogel) and the CDU stood well ahead of the opposition parties in the national opinion polls. As an added bonus for the Chancellor, his bitter rival Franz-Josef Strauss was distracted by internal disputes within the Bavarian CSU as the CSU deputies Franz Handlos and Eberhard Voigt established a small breakaway party — the Republican Party — in opposition to Strauss's personalised style of leadership.[2]

Chancellor Kohl's position of dominance did not, however, last for long. From November 1983, two unfortunate scandals rocked the new administration — the 'Kiessling affair' and the Flick corruption case.

*The Kiessling Affair.* This controversy, although producing a barrage of adverse publicity for the Chancellor, was of only short-term consequence for the government. It had its roots in defence minister Manfred Wörner's dismissal of the deputy NATO commander, General Gunther Kiessling, on 31 December 1983 as a result of a series of counter-intelligence reports which had suggested that Kiessling was a homosexual who posed a serious security risk. Subsequent press and Bundestag investigations showed, however, these reports to be grossly inaccurate and that Kiessling may well have been 'framed' by officers opposed to his policy stance. A fierce political row developed, with the SPD opposition demanding that Kiessling be re-instated and that Wörner should resign as a matter of honour. Helmut Kohl rejected these demands and remained fiercely loyal to Wörner, his close and

---

[1] The November 1979 NATO decision envisaged the stationing of 464 Cruise and 108 Pershing-II ground launched medium-range nuclear missiles in West Germany from the winter of 1983 as part of a major arms modernisation programme. West Germany alone was to deploy Pershing-II missiles which, being able to reach the Soviet Union in fifteen minutes compared to the two hours taken by the Cruise, represented a unique threat to the USSR.

[2] The new Republican Party, although describing itself as a 'conservative-liberal party', aligned itself towards the far-right of the political spectrum, supporting lower taxes for businesses, compulsory military service and the use of plebiscites.

longstanding foreign and defence policy adviser, fearing that, if Wörner left the cabinet, Franz-Josef Strauss would make a bid to gain the defence portfolio. Kohl thus eventually settled upon a fudged, compromise solution in which General Kiessling was re-instated and publicly exonerated, before retiring early with full military honours in April 1984, while Manfred Wörner was retained at the defence ministry. This was not, however, a popular decision and Kohl's uncertain handling of this crisis cast grave doubts over the leadership qualities of the new Chancellor.

This crisis was soon, however, overshadowed by the broader and far more serious Flick scandal which concerned the financing of political parties and which tarnished the reputation of both the FDP and the CDU and which even impugned the integrity of the Chancellor himself.

*Party Finance and the Flick Scandal.* In the modern West German state, an attempt has been made to give political parties independence from the unhealthy pressures exerted by business and labour interest groups. Generous state financial support totalling more than DM 132 million (in 1980) has thus been given, through the subsidy of DM 3.5 per federal vote and DM 1.5 for each vote gained in a Land election contest.[1] State finance has not, however, gone all the way towards rendering parties independent of outside interests. State finance provides only a third of party revenue, the rest has had to be raised, as in other countries, from members and outside donors. The SPD, which pioneered the modern party form, relies overwhelmingly upon the collection of party membership dues: for the FDP, CDU and CSU it is business firms which provide the bulk of party funds (38%, 26% and 36% respectively). These donations have, however, led the parties into controversial and murky waters. Donor companies have sought to keep their contributions secret, while the political parties have looked for tax exemption on such 'gifts'. Such wishes ran up, however, against the 1967 Party Law (amended in 1981), which required the source of all large donations to be declared and which only granted tax immunity to contributions of less than DM 1 800. To circumvent these inconvenient regulations, the political parties, most prominently the FDP and CDU, thus established secretive 'front organisations' claiming charitable status.

A blind eye was initially turned to these illicit operations, but in the later 1970s it was decided that a thorough reform of the Party

[1] Raised to DM 5 from 1984.

51

Law should be effected to remove the need for such clandestine activities by finally granting tax immunity to large company donations. As part of this 'cleaning up' process, a series of investigations were made into the hundreds of existing cases of alleged tax evasion and it was during such enquiries in 1981 that a large tangled web of suspicious dealings involving the huge Flick industrial corporation and key figures within the FDP and the CDU was uncovered. Month by month, new revelations were leaked to the German public by the crusading weekly *Der Spiegel*, building up what became known as the 'Flick Scandal' into a West German 'Watergate' which tarnished the reputation of key figures within the ruling coalition, including the Chancellor himself.

The first damaging exposure occurred in March 1982, when it was revealed that the FDP's federal economics minister, Dr Otto Lambsdorff, and his predecessor, Dr Hans Friderichs, had granted the Flick corporation tax exemptions worth DM 800 million in connection with the company's DM 2 billion sale of its 29% stake in Daimler-Benz in return for a donation of DM 0.5 million to the straitened FDP's party coffers. Throughout 1983, *Der Spiegel* leaked further details concerning these dealings. Helmut Kohl at first reacted to this gathering scandal by attempting, in January 1984, to push through a bill which would grant tax deductions of 50% to political contributions up to specified limits. He went further in May 1984 and tried to extend an amnesty to those involved in past political-fund tax evasions. However, such was the wave of criticism from the opposition SPD and Green parties and from the West German media that Kohl was forced eventually to abandon this bill.

During 1984 the Flick affair ticked away like a time-bomb under the governing coalition, before it finally exploded during the summer and autumn. First, Otto Lambsdorff was forced to resign in June 1984 when a date for his trial was finally set. Then, on 25 October 1984, Rainer Barzel, the former CDU chairman who was currently Bundestag president (speaker), stepped down after it was revealed that between 1973 and 1979 he had secretly accepted DM 1.7 million from the Flick company on behalf of his party.[1] Two weeks later, in November 1984, the scandal directly touched

[1] Barzel was replaced as Bundestag president in November 1984 by Kohl's close aide Philipp Jenninger, with Wolfgang Schäuble, the former CDU-CSU Bundestag floor leader, being inducted as the new head of the Chancellery and eighteenth member of the federal cabinet.

Helmut Kohl, who admitted before a Bundestag investigating committee that he had received DM 140 000 from Flick on behalf of the CDU when serving as minister-president of the Rhineland-Palatinate during the mid-1970s. Kohl stated, however, that these contributions had been purely political, with no conditions attached, and he denied knowledge of any deliberate tax evasion by his Land party's 'charitable research foundation'.

Chancellor Kohl's apparently candid testimony temporarily took the heat out of a 'scandal' which had been blown up out of all proportion by the West German media: it remaining unclear, for example, whether any substantive political favours had been granted in return for Flick's donations. The 'Flick scandal' had nevertheless served to seriously undermine public respect for the major 'system parties' and to encourage popular cynicism. It particularly harmed the FDP and it lowered the standing of Helmut Kohl, whose indecision during this long running crisis led to him being termed the 'Do-Nothing Chancellor' by *Der Spiegel*. Only the anti-establishment Greens profited from these proceedings.

Tainted by the Flick scandal and faced with still high levels of unemployment and only fragile economic recovery, support for the CDU declined substantially during 1984 and 1985. In the old industrial Länder of Hesse, Saarland and North-Rhine Westphalia, which bore the brunt of the contemporary recession, the CDU vote collapsed during the state elections of this period. The party's defeat in Saarland (March 1985) — control of which reverted back to the SPD — was of particular significance. It meant that Franz-Josef Strauss, with his five Bavarian seats, now held the balance of power in the Bundesrat.[1] The rightwing CSU's voice within the federal coalition was thus considerably strengthened. This occurred just at the time when influential figures within the CDU, including its general-secretary and campaign manager for the 1987 Bundestag election, Heiner Geissler, were seeking to move the party back towards a more centrist and interventionist policy course, so that the crucial support of blue-collar workers could be regained.

In April 1983, the newly elected CDU-CSU-FDP coalition, had looked set for more than a decade in office, dominating both the Bundestag and the Bundesrat. Less than two years later the future of the party and Chancellor Kohl appeared far less certain. Criticism from the Chancellor's coalition partners and from the conservative

[1] In May 1985 the SPD held 18 votes in the Bundesrat (from North-Rhine Westphalia, Hesse, Hamburg, Bremen and Saarland), the CDU 18 and the CSU 5.

Springer[1] press (*Die Welt and Bild Zeitung*) mounted, calling for more decisive leadership and for conflicting policy changes. In July 1985, the trial of Otto Lambsdorff, Hans Friderichs and Eberhard von Brauchitsch (a former general-manager of the Flick corporation) began. It re-opened the old wounds of the 'Flick scandal' and, set to last more than a year, would keep the issue in the public's mind all the way up to the January 1987 federal election. On top of all these problems came the Tiedge spy scandal of August-September 1985, which directly affected both the interior minister, Friedrich Zimmermann, and the new FDP leader and federal economics minister, Martin Bangemann.

*The Tiedge Spy Scandal.* This spy scandal was the latest in a long running series which have afflicted West Germany since 1948. It was, however, one of the most serious. West Germany, with its open-door attitude towards its eastern neighbour, its lingering desire for re-unification and its concern for open-government and the protection of civil rights against state interference, has been a fertile ground for Eastern Bloc spies. Marcus Wolf, the talented East German spy chief who finally retired in 1987, is alleged to have established a network of 30 000 agents in West Germany, many of whom found employment as secretaries working in government departments in Bonn. The West German security forces established the Office for the Protection of the Constitution (*Bundesamt für Verfassungsschutz* — BFV) as a counter-intelligence agency in an attempt to break into and uncover this spy network and it was Hans-Joachim Tiedge who headed a key section of this organisation during the early 1980s. Tiedge, a 19-stone alcoholic, faced increasing personal problems after his wife died mysteriously in July 1982 and amassed debts in excess of £60 000. On 19 August 1985 he defected to East Germany as a means of escaping these problems. He brought with him vital intelligence information and agency lists, but, more importantly, his defection led to the unearthing of an extensive network of spies within key government departments, including Sonja Luneberg, who had worked as a secretary for the FDP, serving Martin Bangemann (the new FDP leader and economics minister) for 12 years; Margarete Höke, who had worked as a secretary to successive federal Presidents for 21

---

[1]Axel Springer, the press magnate who controlled 25% of West Germany's national daily newspaper circulation and who was strongly supportive of the CDU, the free-market economy, the peaceful re-unification of Germany and reconciliation with Israel, and who fervently opposed communism and Ostpolitik, died on 22 September 1985 at the age of 73.

years; and Herta-Astrid Willner, who had worked within the Chancellery in a department dealing with domestic security and nuclear power.

The Tiedge scandal precipitated calls by the SPD for the resignation of the Interior Minister, Friedrich Zimmermann — since 1974 and 1978 Willy Brandt and the SPD defence minister, Georg Leber, had resigned as a matter of honour when the East German spies Günter Guillaume and Renate Lutze had been unmasked. However, Zimmermann refused to tender his resignation. Instead, Heribert Hellenberoich, the former head of the BFV and the new chief of the BND (*Bundesnachrichtendienst*) foreign espionage service, who had been aware of Tiedge's personal problems for several months but had not informed Zimmermann, was sacked on 28 August 1985. The ability of Friedrich Zimmermann to remain in office despite this scandal was another example of the authority and independence of individual ministers when drawn from coalition party partners in the West German system of government. Zimmermann, who only two months previously had openly criticised Kohl for his weak leadership and had forced a controversially tough law and order package on the government, was no personal friend of the Chancellor. He could, however, count on the firm support of Franz-Josef Strauss and his CSU colleagues who, with 53 seats, held the balance of power in Bundestag and who played a key role in the Bundersrat. Zimmerman, like foreign minister Genscher, was secure in his post until the next Machtwechsel.

By the autumn of 1985, however, the next Machtwechsel appeared unusually imminent. Chancellor Kohl, despite his cheerful, unruffled exterior, had emerged as the least popular West German Chancellor for more than two decades and it was becoming seriously questioned whether he would be chosen to lead the party into the 1987 federal election. Opinion polls showed that only 12% of those asked preferred Helmut Kohl as Chancellor to other names suggested, for example his liberal-minded finance minister, Gerhard Stoltenberg, or Lothar Späth, the successful and innovative minister-president of Baden-Württemberg, and that only 31% of the West German public believed that Kohl was doing a good job as Chancellor.

Things failed to improve for the Chancellor during the spring of 1986 as his involvement in the 'Flick scandal' was re-examined by the public prosecutor after the Green Party's MP, Otto Schily, filed a legal suit claiming that Kohl had lied to the Land and Bundestag investigating committees in November 1984. Matters were further compounded for the CDU-CSU-FDP coalition by the continued revelations of the Lambsdorff trial[1]; by the irruption of a corruption scandal in West Berlin which forced the resignation in April 1986 of the CDU deputy mayor and two local ministers (including one from the FDP); by intra-coalition wrangles over foreign and domestic policy; and by the alienation of trade unionists, as a result of its proposed new labour legislation, and of farmers, who felt that the government had not been giving them enough financial support. Then, on 26 April 1986, 800 miles east of Bonn, occurred the devastating nuclear accident at the Chernobyl nuclear power station in the Soviet Union which shocked the West German people, radically re-arranged the political agenda and boded ill for the pro-nuclear CDU. The CDU, not surprisingly in such circumstances, polled poorly in local elections in Schleswig-Holstein in March 1986 and figures showed that it had lost 12 000 members during the previous year. Its prospects in the general election, due ten months hence, thus appeared to be in doubt. The party still held a plurality of support over the SPD, but its overall success in January 1987 would very much depend upon the relative performances of the two minority parties which might hold the balance of power — the FDP and the Greens.

## The FDP — policy shifts and public disfavour

The FDP emerged from the March 1983 federal election weakened and divided. However, during the following months the party consolidated around a more conservative policy programme which stressed economic 'laissez faire' liberalism — involving deregulation, intensified market competition, privatisation and a thinned down public sector — rather than 'social liberalism', as the North-Rhine Westphalia, Lower Saxony and Hesse based wing of the party gained ideological ascendancy. The FDP sought now to win over the young, mobile professional voter to add to its traditional clientele of the self-employed and the marginal farmer. Such FDP ideas formed an important input into the economic programme of the CDU-CSU-FDP coalition. However, attempts to build up support for this 'new liberalism' were dashed by the 'Flick scandal', which directly affected the programme's chief architect, Otto Lambsdorff.

[1] The CSU leader, Franz-Josef Strauss, and SPD former leader, Willy Brandt, were also accused of receiving funds from the Flick corporation during this trial.

The standing of the party, already lowered by its political deceptions during September-October 1982, plunged once more with this new crisis. At first the party did not fare too badly. It lost its voice in the Bremen assembly following fresh elections in September 1983, but regained, with the aid of CDU 'ticket-splitting', its representation in the Hesse Landtag. However, in the June 1984 European Parliament elections, when only one vote — for a regional party list — was available, the party fared disastrously. It fell below the 5% electoral hurdle and thus failed to obtain a voice in the European Parliament to which the party was so passionately committed.

This disastrous result finally persuaded the increasingly unpopular Hans-Dietrich Genscher to announce his resignation as party leader after February 1985 — Genscher would still continue, however, as foreign minister, ensuring the continuance of Ostpolitik detente. He was replaced by Martin Bangemann, a former Euro-MP and the new economics minister, who stood on the free-market wing of the party. This change of leadership failed, however, to heal the divisions within the party: during Bangemann's inaugural speech to the party's February 1985 Saarbrücken conference one quarter of the delegates left while he was speaking. Nevertheless, there was evidence of a limited revival in party fortunes under the new leadership during 1985 — the party returning creditable performances in the Länder elections in West Berlin, the Saarland and North-Rhine-Westphalia — before the 'Tiedge scandal' and the opening of the Lambsdorff trial in August 1985 threatened to damage the party once again. Nevertheless, the much trumpeted demise of the balance-holding FDP had failed to materialise.

Tensions and differences did, however, grow within the ruling coalition, particularly between the FDP and CSU during 1985-6. These two parties, while united in their support for a radical, de-regulatory 'liberal' approach to economic affairs, found themselves at odds over foreign policy — particularly over the issues of Ostpolitik, West Germany's involvement in work on the American 'Star Wars' project and the imposition of sanctions against South Africa[1] — and over the new anti-libertarian law and order measures introduced at home. In May 1986, the coalition was further strained when FDP rank-and-file delegates, influenced by Chernobyl,

[1] The FDP supported sanctions against South Africa and were wary of participation in the 'Star Wars' (space-based anti-ballistic missile system) project. The CSU took a directly contrary line.

revolted against the party leadership and supported a series of anti-nuclear motions at the party's pre-election conference at Hanover in direct opposition to government policy.[1] Despite these differences, however, the coalition held together during 1986, being helped by the consensual bridge-building work of the moderate, cross-class CDU and its leader Helmut Kohl, and by a realistion among senior figures within the FDP that, at present, there remained no alternative but to remain members of the incumbent administration.

## The Greens — The pains of political maturity

The Greens continued to make electoral advances in the years following the March 1983 federal election. Their most spectacular successes were in Baden-Württemberg (March 1984) and West Berlin (March 1985) — two areas with a distinctive radical tradition — where they gained 8.3% and 10.6% of the poll, and in the June 1984 elections to the European Parliament, when they captured 8% of the national vote. By 1984, with seats in six Länder, the Greens had moved ahead of the FDP as West Germany's third party.

During 1983, the heated national debate over the stationing of Pershing-II missiles and the demonstrations of the 'hot autumn' — which involved more than 900 000 at Hamburg, Bonn, Stuttgart and West Berlin — gave the party a high national profile. However, once these missiles had been deployed the peace movement lost momentum, although the proposed deployment of Cruise missiles at Hasselbach in 1986 provided another target to campaign against. Instead, it was the environmental issues of nuclear power and acid rain which gained increasing importance for the party from 1984. On these issues, the Greens had considerable success in persuading the CDU-CSU-FDP government — concerned with the destruction of forests in its southern German heartland — to take decisive action. Restrictions were now placed upon sulphur dioxide discharges from coal-fired power stations, incentives were granted to purchasers of vehicles with catalytic convertors (which reduce exhaust emissions) and legislation was passed for the introduction of lead-free petrol by 1989. During this same period, both CDU and

[1] At the 23-25 May Hanover conference motions were carried calling for a 'review' of the need for and safety of nuclear reprocessing at the Wackersdorf plant being built in Bavaria (a project strongly supported by Franz-Josef Strauss); a review of the fast-breeder reactor project at Kalkar (North-Rhine-Westphalia) near the Dutch border; and a freeze on the building of new nuclear power plants until the causes of the Chernobyl accident had been fully assessed.

SPD administrations within the Länder were also goaded into delaying the execution of projected nuclear power programmes by the activities of the Green movement.

However, while the Greens were able to influence the policy debate on environmental issues, as a party they became divided over which political direction to adopt — one of collaboration or one of confrontation with the existing 'system parties'. The Greens presented themselves to the electorate as an informal, broad-church, anti-establishment and anti-elitist 'new party'. The entry of its representatives into the Landtage and Bundestag served to shock the existing 'system parties'. Green deputies were young (average age 40), an unusually high proportion (more than 40%) were female and they dressed informally in jerseys, jeans and T-shirts. They acted as mandated delegates to their rank-and-file membership; they stepped down in midterm in favour of understudies on the party list, in accordance with the party's unique 'rotation principle'; and they drew only a quarter of their official salary (ploughing back the remainder into the party treasury).

However, differences gradually developed between elected Green delegates and the rank-and-file over whether to persist with this informal strategy or whether to weld the party into a more efficient, streamlined and 'professional' movement. Key figures within the party's leadership, including Otto Schily (a former defence lawyer to the Baader-Meinhof terrorist gang), General Gert Bastian (a former member of the CDU) and Joschka Fischer (a former *Sponti* student activist during the 1960s who was now the Greens' Bundestag floor leader), favoured the adoption of a more pragmatic and responsible stance of working within the existing political institutions and of engaging in coalitions with the major parties at state level to achieve particular goals. They became termed the *Realos*. In contrast, many of the younger rank-and-file membership, the so-called *Fundis*, disagreed, viewing such an approach as a betrayal of the Greens' 'anti-party' principles. They firmly opposed entering into coalitions with the 'system parties', preferring an antagonistic, nuisance-making role, and pressed hard for continuance of the 'rotation principle'.[1]

[1] The division between '*Realos*' and '*Fundis*' has been not just generational, but also regional, with urban branches, such as Hamburg and West Berlin, being notoriously radical. They seek to construct 'alternative coalitions' including feminists, squatters, homosexuals, peace activists, environmentalists, single-parents and the disabled and propound Marxist-tinged economic programmes, while rural branches, for example Baden-Württemberg, have been more conservative in their approach to economic and social issues.

The 'Fundis' dominated the Greens' national executive committee and gained initial support from the party's charismatic leader, Petra Kelly, who was situated on the centre-left of the party. At its November 1982 conference at Hagen (Westphalia), the 'Fundis' easily won a motion to maintain the principle of a rotating leadership — Rainer Trampert (a Hamburg trade unionist and an ally of the 'Fundis') replacing Petra Kelly as national chairperson. In March 1984, the 'rotation principle' was re-affirmed when it was decided to replace six of the Greens' most prominent Bundestag deputies — including Schily (who had gained wide attention for his work on the Flick investigation committee), Kelly, Fischer, Bastian and its anti-nuclear campaigner, Roland Vogt — with a sextumvirate of obscure female 'shadow-deputies' (three teachers, one lecturer, one professor and one nurse). Kelly and Vogt, however, objected to this principle, arguing that it wasted accumulated experience. They pressed instead for deputies to be allowed to continue in office so long as 70% of their Land branch voted in their favour. Such divisions over the 'rotation principle' caused the first major split in the party when General Bastian left the Fraktion in frustration with the amateurish ineptitude of the party's organisation, retaining his Bundestag seat as an independent. A compromise of sorts was eventually arrived at, with 23 new deputies entering the Bundestag for the new session in March 1985, but with the party's principal leaders, Kelly, Vogt and Schily, retaining their seats.[1] The 'Fundis' had, nevertheless, won the major portion of their rotation argument.

At the Länder level, the Greens had to decide what position to adopt when they found themselves holding the balance of power. This occurred in Hamburg between June and December 1982 and in Hesse from September 1982.

In Hamburg, the June 1982 election gave the incumbent SPD government only 55 seats compared with the CDU's 56, and left them dependent on the Greens (with 9 seats) for support. The SPD leader, Klaus Von Dohnanyi, attempted to reach a 'toleration agreement' with the Greens, but the Greens demanded in return the abandonment of the city's nuclear energy programme and the scrapping of planned extensions to Hamburg port. This the SPD

---

[1] They had threatened to sit as independents if they had been forced to rotate their seats. This would have reduced the Greens to only 23 official deputies — insufficient under the West German constitution to qualify as a Bundestag Fraktion. They would thus have lost the right to sit on committees and to draw office and campaign funds from the state.

could not accept. They thus stumbled on until December 1982, before winning an absolute majority of seats in a new election.

In Hesse the September 1982 elections also resulted in a 'hung Landtag', with the Greens' nine deputies holding the balance of power, and 'toleration' negotiations broke down once more when the SPD refused to accede to the Greens' demands to halt plans to expand Frankfurt airport. A new election was called in September 1983, but, in contrast to Hamburg, no decisive result was obtained: the Greens continuing to hold the balance of power following the new contest. Pressure now mounted on the Greens to act responsibly and form a coalition with the SPD in the interests of political stability. The Greens' actions in Hamburg were thus viewed with great interest as indicative of their likely attitude to a possible 'red-green' coalition with the SPD at the federal level if the January 1987 Bundestag election produced a hung parliament.

In June 1984 the centre-right SPD minister-president of Hesse, Holger Börner, following lengthy negotiations, eventually came to a 'toleration agreement' with the Greens at the cost of a number of environmental and budgetary concessions — the SPD agreeing to limit the construction of new motorways, restrict the dumping of chemical waste and stop building new nuclear power stations: the Greens (led by the 'Realo' Karl Kerschgens) assenting in return to tolerate the operation of existing nuclear plants and to lift their opposition to a new runway at Frankfurt airport. However, this loose alliance lasted barely six months before 'Fundis', accusing Kerschgens of a sell-out, withdrew their support in November 1984 after the SPD had failed to cancel plans for two nuclear power stations. Holger Börner made a final attempt to form a coalition in June 1985 when he offered the Greens' Joschka Fischer the state ministry for the environment and energy — although ultimate control of nuclear energy policy was to be wielded by the SPD economics minister — if the Land party would agree in return to ensure the passage of the state budgets between 1985 and 1987. The Greens remained divided over whether to opt for coalition or to reject collaboration — their 22 June conference at Hagen passing an equivocal resolution — but, following weeks of tortuous negotiations, Kerschgens finally agreed to the arrangement in September 1985. A month later, on 27 October 1985, the pact was approved by a two-thirds majority at a special Land conference at Neu-Isenberg and on 12 December 1985 Joschka Fischer (37), wearing jeans and tennis shoes, was sworn in as environment minister in Wiesbaden, becoming the first Green to hold state office in West Germany. [1] Fischer's appointment, which sent tremors through the Hesse financial and industrial community, was seen as a possible precursor to a coalition at the federal level with the SPD in 1987. However, the majority of Greens still remained bitterly opposed to such collaboration and at the party's annual national conference in Offenburg in December 1985 the 'Fundis' remained dominant at executive committee level.

By the autumn of 1985, however, the Green movement appeared to have passed its peak. Party membership was stagnant at 40 000 and the Greens' electoral popularity was on the wane: in the North-Rhine-Westphalia state election of May 1985 it gained only 4.8% support (compared to 8.6% in local elections there in October 1984) and in Saarland two months earlier it polled only 2.5%. The anti-growth economic policies of the party failed, in particular, to attract blue-collar workers in these industrial states. The Green Party was also being forced to clarify its ambiguous position on a wide range of issues and present a coherent national programme. This created internal dissent as a number of the variegated interests within the party were disappointed with the direction chosen. The issue of coalition with the SPD was the most fundamental question.

The Greens also now found its appeal with younger voters, who had been attracted by its freshness and nuisance-making value, declining, as the public began to grow tired of the party's organised chaos, and it found that many of the defence and environmental issues for which it had campaigned were now being adopted by the major 'system parties', which took on a greener hue during the early 1980s. Within the CDU for example, Lothar Späth, the minister-president of Baden-Württemberg, pursued a dynamic anti-pollution programme and even in conservative Bavaria the CSU, prompted by anxious local farmers, showed a genuine concern for the condition of the state's decaying forests. It was, however, the SPD, which came out against the installation of Pershing-II missiles in November 1983 and which was now being driven forward by a group of new environmentally conscious state leaders — the most prominent being the eco-socialist Oskar Lafontaine, leader in the Saarland — which was making the strongest inroads into the Green vote. The Greens had certainly tapped a new section of the electorate attracted by the new style of politics it offered and by its alternative political and economic vision. However, this segment

[1] The Greens, in addition, were given the post of state secretary for women's affairs in Hesse.

remained small. The survival of the party in the Bundestag after 1987 began, from the autumn of 1985, to appear doubtful.

In the spring of 1986, however, the Greens, who had been engaged in a determined series of demonstrations at the sites of the proposed Brokdorf and Wackersdorf nuclear power and reprocessing plants and at the Hasselbach Cruise missile base, were suddenly revivified by the numbing nuclear catastrophe at Chernobyl. This accident, which led to the contamination of 1000 sq kms of Russian farmland and to momentary panic in West Germany as a radioactive cloud swept overhead, stunned the German people and suddenly transformed the political agenda. The popular concern was even greater than that aroused by the construction of the Berlin Wall in August 1961. Not surprisingly, therefore, national support for the Greens suddenly surged from a level of 6% to more than 8%, with the protest rallies called by the party at Wackersdorf and Brokdorf in June and July 1986 being unusually well attended. Chernobyl, however, had a second and less salutary impact on the Green movement, radicalising it to a dangerous degree. This was seen most visibly at the Wackersdorf and Brokdorf demonstrations, which grew increasingly violent, reaching riot proportions in Hamburg on 8 June 1986. It was, also, most evident at the special pre-election conference called by the national party at Hanover on 16-19 May at which, with the 'Fundis' in the ascendant, a hardline party programme was adopted calling for the immediate cessation of nuclear power generation, withdrawal from NATO, removal of Pershing-II and Cruise missiles and the disbandment of West Germany's Border Guards, army and intelligence forces.[1] Such radicalisation pushed the Greens further beyond the borders of conventional West German politics and placed new, and seemingly insurmountable obstacles, in the way of a future 'red-green' federal coalition with the SPD.

## The SPD — which road back to power?

The SPD remained divided throughout 1983 by the debate over the stationing of Pershing-II missiles. Helmut Schmidt and the centre-right saw the need to accept these missiles to show solidarity with West Germany's NATO allies. However, the party's influential chairman, Willy Brandt, came out against deployment — speaking at the huge Bonn peace rally on 22 October — and was supported

---

[1] The Hanover conference did, however, bring one victory for the party's 'Realos', with the abandonment of the midterm Bundestag deputy 'rotation principle'.

by the bulk of party activists at a special conference in Cologne on 18 November 1983, when the party voted by 383 to 14 (with three abstentions) against acceptance. This historic decision represented the first major breach in the all-party defence consensus in West Germany since 1959.

The decision established the SPD as a clear centre-left party, with Willy Brandt its controlling figure supported by a left-dominated executive committee. Helmut Schmidt, who had spoken against the 18 November decision, announced shortly afterwards that he would not be standing for the Bundestag in the next federal election or for any leading party post. (In May 1984 he resigned as one of the party's two deputy chairmen to be replaced by Hans-Jöchen Vogel). Herbert Werner, the stern 77 year old Bundestag floor leader — a passionate left-wing supporter of detente and re-unification — had also stepped down a year earlier to be similarly replaced in his post by Hans-Jöchen Vogel. Control of the SPD thus now passed to a new generation of leaders — under the guardianship of Willy Brandt — as the party sought a new sense of direction.

The party remained unclear as to what this direction should be during 1983 and 1984. The SPD drifted leftward in its defence stance, though still remaining committed to NATO, and became more environmentally conscious, as it toyed with the idea of a 'red-green' majority seeking coalition with the increasingly popular Green Party. At the state level, however, individual party leaders pursued differing programmes — centre-right (in West Berlin under the former defence minister, Hans Apel), centre (in Hamburg, Hesse, Bremen and North-Rhine-Westphalia), radical-left (in the Saarland under the anti-NATO Oskar Lafontaine, in Baden/Württemberg under Erhard Eppler and in Schleswig-Holstein under Björn Engholm) — with varying degrees of success. The SPD's policy position was thus kept necessarily vague during these years.

At home, however, the CDU-CSU-FDP coalition's failure to reduce unemployment, particularly in the older industrialised north, presented an issue around which the party could unite and attract wider electoral support. The SPD pushed for an expansionary and interventionist economic strategy and picked up increasing support from blue-collar groups for this programme. This was first apparent in the Hamburg and Hesse elections of September 1983 and in the Munich municipality election of March 1984 (when the SPD won the mayorship for the first time since 1972-8). During 1984 the party benefited from the 'Flick scandal' and by the spring of 1985 the advance of the SPD was spectacular.

It regained control of the Saarland, ending more than a decade of CDU rule, and capatured a record 52% of the poll in North-Rhine Westphalia, the key barometer region in West Germany which contained almost a third of the total electorate.[1]

In their victor in North-Rhine-Westphalia, the 54-year-old Johannes Rau, the SPD had appeared to have finally found the vote-winning personality which they had missed since the departure of Helmut Schmidt. Rau, the devout son of a Protestant pastor who was married to an attractive 29-year-old wife, and had a small family, proved to be a popular and engaging centrist leader very much in the mould of Helmut Schmidt — down to his love for wearing a 'student cap' during election campaigns.[2] He had already acted as a party deputy chairman since April 1982 and in September 1985 Rau agreed to stand as chancellor-candidate in January 1987 if endorsed by the SPD conference in Nuremberg in August 1986. Rau was duly endorsed, replacing the uninspiring stop-gap Hans-Jöchen Vogel, who remained nevertheless as the party's Bundestag leader. During the autumn of 1985 and spring of 1986 Rau made a strong impression on the West German public and engaged in well publicised visits to Moscow, Paris, London and Washington. He still remained politically 'raw', being prone to making policy gaffes, but his warm, optimistic and intuitive manner enabled him to open up a ten point lead over Chancellor Kohl in opinion polls during the spring of 1986.

Rau's accession to the leadership also strengthened the party's right wing in the intra-party policy battle. Leftwingers still pressed for the adoption of a radical defence programme — some, for example Lafontaine, favouring complete withdrawal from NATO and the immediate removal of Cruise and Pershing-II missiles;

[1] The SPD's disastrous performance in the West Berlin election of March 1985 — picking up only 32% of the poll in a traditional party stronghold — can be attributed to factional divisions within the local party, its unpopularity as a result of a series of corruption scandals and the successful administrative records of the CDU mayors Richard Von Weizsäcker (who left to become federal president in May 1984) and Eberhard Diepgen.

[2] Rau, born at Wuppertal in January 1931, first worked as a salesman for a church publishing company and emerged as an early supporter of the pacifist, SPD-convert, Gustav Heinemann. He was elected into the North-Rhine-Westphalia Landtag in 1958 and served as mayor of Wuppertal (1970-8) and Land minister for science and research during the 1970s, before rising to become minister-president of North-Rhine-Westphalia in September 1978. In the state elections of both May 1980 and May 1985 Rau succeeded in successively increasing the SPD's share of the Land vote.

others, including Brandt and Bahr, seeking to give new emphasis to Ostpolitik with the ultimate aim of creating a neutralised, nuclear-free central Europe[1] — for a curb on nuclear power generation and for the formation of a 'red-green' federal alliance. They were forced to give way, however, to Johannes Rau, who sought to regain the political middle-ground through the pursuit of a compromise, centrist programme of firm attachment to NATO, the 'freezing' of Cruise and Pershing-II missile deployment, opposition to the 'Star Wars' project, the phased reduction of nuclear power and the re-emphasis of traditional 'bread and butter' economic and 'social justice' issues, but which rejected the possibility of a future federal coalition with the Greens.

## Party politics on the eve of the 1987 federal election

During the spring of 1986, faced with the 'Rau Factor', Chernobyl and the perjury allegations against Chancellor Kohl, victory for the CDU-CSU-FDP alliance in the January 1987 federal election was very much in doubt. The ruling coalition also faced the real prospect of defeat in the Land election in Lower Saxony in June 1986 and the loss of its Bundesrat majority. This defeat was, however, averted as the fortunes of the CDU-CSU-FDP coalition were dramatically revived by the events of the summer and autumn of 1986.

First, on 21 and 30 May 1986, the Koblenz and Bonn public prosecutors terminated their investigations into the 'Kohl perjury case' and exonerated the Chancellor fully of all charges of deception.[2] This boost to the ruling coalition was supported, secondly, by strong signs of improvement in the West German economy, which now began to boast a zero rate of inflation and a buoyant level of industrial growth which was at last making some dent on the unemployment total. This provided the opportunity for the government to introduce major tax cuts and to raise farm subsidies (in May 1986) by DM 500 million in an attempt to win back the support of previously alienated middle class and agricul-

[1] In the summer of 1985 Egon Bahr signed a draft treaty with the East German communist party banning chemical weapons from German soil as an initial step in this new strategy and in October 1986 the two German socialist parties jointly called for the creation of a 94-mile wide demilitarised nuclear-free zone either side of their respective borders.

[2] In a separate, but partly related case, the Federal Constitutional Court also finally ruled on changes to the party finance law in July 1986, allowing for individuals or companies to make tax-free political contributions of up to DM 100 000 per annum.

tural groups. A third, and more surprising, boost to the government's fortunes was provided by the Chernobyl disaster. Chernobyl initially lost the government considerable support, but slowly the Kohl administration began to profit from the clear stance it took on the divisive issue of nuclear power. The government made clear its commitment to nuclear safety by calling for a new series of safety checks on the country's reactors and establishing a new environment ministry in June 1986[1]. It refused, however, to countenance a retreat from nuclear power, viewing it as essential to the maintenance of the nation's industrial pre-eminence. This stance reflected the views of many non-committed voters who were concerned with the growing radicalism and violence of the anti-nuclear movement. It proved sufficient for the CDU to narrowly retain, with FDP support, control over the Lower Saxony assembly after the crucial elections of 15 June 1986.

The result in Lower Saxony (see Appendix B), despite a significant 6% fall in the CDU vote and a reduction in the CDU-FDP's overall majority from eleven seats to a bare majority of one, came as an immense relief to the ruling coalition. It ended speculation concerning the replacement of Helmut Kohl (56) as the CDU chancellor-candidate for January 1987 and it gave a boost to Martin Bangemann's leadership of the FDP. The poll result came as the greatest blow to the Greens, whose share of the vote rose by only 0.6%. The voters in this bench-mark state clearly became alarmed by the mounting extremism of the ecological party and decided instead to support the SPD, whose local leader, Gerhard Schröder (42), promised radicalism but refused to countenance a 'red-green' coalition. The SPD thus won over many of Lower Saxony's floating voters and raised its share of the state poll by an impressive 5.6%

Chancellor-candidate Johannes Rau declared himself buoyed by the Lower Saxony result, which he hoped would give a 'good following wind' for the January 1987 federal contest in which the SPD sought to achieve an unprecedented outright electoral majority. Rau was also cheered by the outcome of the party's national conference held at Nuremberg in August 1986 in which he gained warm and unified backing from the party's elder statesmen

---

[1]This new, nineteenth, federal ministry (termed the ministry of the environment, nature conservation and reactor safety), which was headed by Walter Wallmann (53), the popular mayor of Frankfurt and Land chairman of the CDU in Hesse, took powers away from Friedrich Zimmermann's hard-nosed interior ministry. In October 1986, following rigorous safety checks, the new ministry sanctioned the opening of the Brokdorf pressurised water reactor in Schleswig-Holstein.

and acceptance of a radical, but fudged, centre-left manifesto policy programme. In its motion on defence, the conference pledged West Germany's continued support for its alliance with the United States, while at the same time calling for the withdrawal of both American and Soviety medium-range nuclear weapons from Europe (the 'zero option') and an end to West German participation in the 'Star Wars' project. On the issue of nuclear power, the party pledged itself to halt the construction of all new plants, but sought, not the immediate closure, but rather the phasing-out over a ten year timespan of stations already operating, and a gradual switch towards a new conservation and coal-based energy strategy. Finally, on the domestic issues of unemployment and social justice, on which Rau himself placed overriding emphasis during his 90-minute keynote address, the party promised, if elected to power, to introduce a major new job investment programme, which would be financed by tax surcharges on high wage earners; to continue the move towards a shorter working week; to cut the taxes of lower and middle income earners; to improve the opportunities for women; and to reduce social divisions within the country: Rau declaring his intention to govern as a 'Chancellor of all the citizens'.

Despite the success of Nuremberg, the SPD's repeated assertions that, with a further push, it could achieve a single party majority within the Bundesrat grew increasingly fanciful as 1986 progressed. The opinion poll rating of Chancellor Kohl steadily improved as a consequence of his exculpation from the 'Flick scandal' in May and the continuing growth in the West German economy, while the rating for Johannes Rau began to dip as political commentators and senior party colleagues, most prominently Klaus Bölling, began to question his lack of federal administrative experience and to closely and critically examine his Land record and imprecise policy prescriptions. Matters worsened for the SPD from September 1986 with news of the collapse of the huge, trade union linked, *Neue Heimat* (New Home) low-cost housing syndicate amid allegations of gross mismanagement and financial irregularities.[1] Although not itself directly involved in the running of the Neue Heimat concern, the failure of what had been seen as one of the shining lights of the

---

[1] Neue Heimat, which was owned by the DGB's industrial holding company BGAG (*Beteiligungsgesellschaft für Gemeinwirtschaft*), had been formed in 1954 to provide cheap housing for the poor and underprivileged. In return for agreeing to invest 96% of its profits in housing, it had been given generous tax concessions and by 1980 owned 330 000 homes and controlled an additional 240 000. Since 1980, however, the company had fallen prey to unwise property speculations.

1970s, Brandt-Schmidt era, *Gemeinwirtschaft* (social economy) approach to economic and social affairs seriously disillusioned SPD supporters, particularly blue-collar voters. This was reflected in the 12 October 1986 Bavaria state election, where the SPD vote, despite energetic leadership by Land Chairman, Karl Heinz Hiersmann, fell by 4.4% and the party recorded its worst ever result since 1949. A month later, on 9 November 1986, the SPD polled even more disastrously in its traditional stronghold of Hamburg. In the northern city state, which was the headquarters for Neue Heimat, the SPD's vote declined by almost 10% as the party was beaten into second place by the CDU and forced to form a minority administration with Greens and CDU 'toleration'.

In both elections one of the most notable features of the polls was the low turnout — in Bavaria only 70.3% of the Land electorate voted compared with 78% in 1982, in Hamburg only 77.2% compared with 84% in 1982[1] — as many blue-collar, core SPD supporters stayed at home. The other significant feature was the sharp rise in support for the Green Party, which entered the Landtag, with a 7.5% vote, for the first time in traditionally conservative Bavaria and which, fielding an all-female Land list and campaigning for the immediate closure of all nuclear power stations, significantly increased its strength in the Hamburg *Bürgerschaft* (city parliament), capturing 10.4% of the vote. The party benefited from public concern over a major accident at the Sandoz chemical factory in Basel (Switzerland) on 1 November 1986, which resulted in the widespread and lasting pollution of the Rhine river, and from local opposition to the Wackersdorf (Bavaria) and Brokdorf (near Hamburg) projects. It also profited from splits within the ranks of the SPD, as more radical elements, critical of the centrist Rau's fudged policy programme and his continued refusal to countenance a 'red-green' coalition, transferred support to the ecologist party.

The dismal showing of the SPD in Hamburg produced consternation and disarray in party ranks, with its chief spokesman Wolfgang Clement tendering his resignation and senior colleagues publicly voicing recognition that victory in January 1987 was no longer possible. Indeed, with the national opinion poll rating of the SPD having fallen from a level of 44% to one of 35-38% since the autumn of 1985, party chairman Willy Brandt declared that a figure

---

[1] In 1982 the SPD vote in Hamburg had, however, been unduly inflated by contemporary sympathy for deposed Chancellor and 'local hero', Helmut Schmidt.

of 43% for the party in January 1987 would be a 'good result'. Chancellor-candidate Johannes Rau soldiered on out of a sense of duty, but victory for the right-coalition had become certain as the election campaign entered its final straight in December 1986 and January 1987.

## The January 1987 Federal Election

By the winter of 1986 polls showed the right-coalition to hold a level of national support of between 52-54%. The crucial question for the coalition's members was, however, how this support would be distributed among the individual parties in January 1987. As in 1983, the debate revolved around two issues: firstly, whether the FDP would once more surmount the 5% federal hurdle; and secondly, if it did, whether the CDU-CSU Fraktion would still be able to achieve a majority of Bundestag seats on their own. Again, as in 1983, it was CSU leader Franz-Josef Strauss who took the lead in encouraging this intra-coalition debate.

The 71-year-old Strauss viewed January 1987 as possibly his last chance of returning to the federal stage as a leading minister, setting his sights on replacing the FDP's Hans-Dietrich Genscher as Vice-Chancellor and foreign minister or, as a second option, taking over from Manfred Wörner as defence minister. He thus began a campaign during the autumn of 1986 which was aimed at discrediting Genscher, by personally interfering in the conduct of foreign affairs and calling into question what he saw as the latter's one-sided policy of Ostpolitik detente and his lukewarm support for the United States. In August 1986, as part of this strategy, Strauss precipitated a diplomatic crisis with neighbouring Austria by brusquely replying to the Austrian President, Kurt Waldheim's, request for the Bavarian Land government to reconsider the Wackersdorf nuclear reprocessing plant project. The crisis had to be resolved by a shuttle-trip by Genscher to Salzburg to smooth ruffled Austrian feathers. Then in September 1986, in an interview with *Welt am Sonntag*, Strauss fiercely criticised Genscher's conduct of foreign affairs and, in particular, his attempt to play mediator between the two superpowers which the Bavarian minister-president likened to 'little Fritz running after the regimental band with his rattle'.

Strauss's actions drew concern from Helmut Kohl and led to the Chancellor's adoption of a more hawkish and conservative image and policy line during the closing months of 1986 in an effort to outflank his rightwing ally. Thus during October 1986 Kohl cautioned the Reagan administration, at that time engaged in arms control negotiations with the Soviet Union in Reykjavik, not to suddenly remove medium-range nuclear missiles from Europe and made plain West Germany's backing of the American 'Star Wars' programme. The Chancellor, in addition, during the autumn of 1986 continued to resist calls for the imposition of economic sanctions against South Africa; took a firm stance against international terrorism; and employed lax and controversial language in October 1986 and later in January 1987 when he likened the Soviet leader Mikhail Gorbachev's public relations skills to those of 'Goebbels' and declared that East Germany held 2000 political prisoners in 'prisons and concentration camps'. More importantly, Helmut Kohl, as the first Chancellor to have lived all his adult life in the democratic Fourth Reich, sought during his campaign speeches between October 1986 and January 1987 to lay to rest the country's Nazi legacy and to give sanction to the espousal of a new, responsible, forward looking national feeling and pride. This theme was given particular emphasis at the CDU's national conference at Mainz on 6-8 October 1986 and at a major pre-election rally at Dortmund in January 1987, when the Chancellor declared that 'Love of fatherland (*Vaterland*) is a virtue that becomes every people, the Germans as well'.

The rightward shift in the CDU-CSU approach to foreign policy was paralleled at home. The two parties' joint manifesto, entitled 'Manifesto for the Future', placed emphasis upon continuing technological modernisation to maintain West Germany as a 'world leader'; on further deregulation, privatisation and tax reductions; and on a firmer approach to law and order and immigration control. This hardening of policy and rhetoric worked to the FDP's advantage, resulting in a rallying of support to the liberal party, which was once more viewed as a vital 'corrective' within the coalition by a public supportive of Hans-Dietrich Genscher's vision of beginning a new 'second phase' of Ostpolitik and detente. Thus, as the election campaign entered its closing weeks the poll rating of the FDP increased markedly and when votes were finally cast on 25 January 1987 the houdini-like third party comfortably surmounted the 5% barrier and recorded its second best national result since 1965, capturing 9.1% of the federal total. (See Table 11).

### Table 11 The January 1987 Bundestag Election
### (Turnout 84.4%)

|  | ('000) Zweitstimmen Votes | (%) Share of Total Vote | Seats |
|---|---|---|---|
| CDU-CSU | 16 923 | 44.3 | 223 |
| SPD | 14 134 | 37.0 | 186 |
| FDP | 3 476 | 9.1 | 46 |
| Greens | 3 171 | 8.3 | 42 |
| NPD | 229 | 0.6 | — |
| Others | 267 | 0.7 |  |
| Total | 38 200 | 100.0 | 497[1] |

[1]The CDU-CSU captured 169 direct Erstimmen consituency seats, the SPD 79.

The CDU-CSU, by contrast, despite polls showing its national rating at 49% during December 1986, found its vote severely squeezed during the final weeks of the campaign, and recorded its lowest share of a Bundestag election poll since 1949. The party's share of the national vote fell by 4.5% and its number of total votes captured by more than two million. Surveys showed that a net 800 000 CDU-CSU voters, particularly those in the southwest and central Rhine regions, switched support to the FDP; 400 000, concentrated in the industrialised north, to the SPD; and more than 100 000 of its votes were drawn away by the extreme-right NPD, whose share of the national vote tripled to 0.6% (the NPD's best national performance since 1972). A further 750 000 former supporters of the conservative alliance chose to stay at home, as the overall electoral turnout slumped to 84.4%, the lowest level since 1949. The rightward shift in the CDU-CSU stance on foreign policy and domestic economic issues was the principal factor explaining the alliance's loss of votes to the FDP and SPD respectively. The largescale abstentions and abnormally low voter turnout was ascribed by psephologists to bitterly cold weather conditions, January 1987 having been the first national election held during winter in the Federal Republic, and to a general lack of interest in what proved to be a dull and predictable campaign, with victory for the incumbent coalition appearing to be certain months in advance. The Kohl team, aware of the dangers of a loss of support as a result of such abstentions, campaigned hard during the closing weeks of the election contest, spending heavily on a media-blitz of advertisements. However, the CDU-CSU's slogans of '*Wieter So Deutschland*' ('Steady Ahead Germany') and '*Zukunft*' ('The Future') proved tepid and uninspiring.

The SPD was even more concerned and disappointed with its national performance in January 1987 than the conservative CDU-CSU, although its overall share of the federal vote fell by only 1.2% and its total number of votes captured by 730 000. The party, while gaining some net support from the CDU and holding firm in the north, where its locally based chancellor-candidate proved to be a popular figure, lost votes on the centre-right to the FDP and suffered a further haemorrhage of support (estimated at 650 000 votes) on the left and among young first-time voters to the ecologist Greens. The party thus achieved its lowest share of the national poll since 1961 (the first election following its renovation at Bad Godesberg). The result could, however, have been far worse for the SPD. At the end of December 1986, a major survey poll by the Allensbach Institute showed the party's national rating standing at the humiliating level of only 32.4%. Support, however, rallied towards chancellor-candidate Rau, who fought a spirited and well mannered campaign, during the closing weeks of the contest.

The most striking performance in January 1987 was, however, the continued rise in the fortunes of the ecologist Green Party. Following a typically unorthodox and largely non-political campaign, termed 'Winter Magic', consisting of music festivals, poetry recitals and demonstrations at nuclear power stations and weapons' sites, the ecologist party succeeded in easily surmounting the 5% electoral hurdle, raising its share of the federal poll by a third (or by one million votes) to a level of 8.3%. The party drew in considerable support from the 3.6 million new first-time voters and from disillusioned former SPD voters. It made advances, however, all across the country, raising its share of the vote in rural Bavaria, for example, by 7.6%. This, taken in conjunction with the fact that it held seats in seven Landtage, meant that the Greens had truly established themselves as a national party and as a permanent fixture in what had become a quadripolar (two major and two minor parties) West German party political system. In addition, the entry of the Greens' deputies into the Bundestag, 57% (i.e. 25) of whom were females, significantly altered the complexion of the lower chamber, doubling the proportion of women in the

Bundestag to a figure of more than 15% and placing women's issues to the forefront of the national agenda. [1]

## Political Developments after the January 1987 Election

### The new Kohl administration: continuity or change?

Chancellor Kohl, despite his rhetorical gestures to the party's right wing, had contested the January 1987 federal election as a man proud and content with the achievements of 1983−7 and who promised no stark policy changes. He pledged instead, under the slogan 'More of the Same', to maintain a steady hand on the tiller and to continue his programme of modernising and streamlining the economy and maintaining West Germany as a loyal pillar in the Atlantic alliance. The strong showing for the FDP helped ensure that Kohl's programme of economic liberalisation, involving the removal of industrial subsidies and support, privatisation, further tax reductions and an overhaul of the welfare system, would continue. It secondly ensured, however, that any thoughts that CDU-CSU rightwingers may have had of abandoning West Germany's Ostopolitik brokerage role between East and West and moving towards a more narrowly partisan alignment with the United States would need to be jettisoned. The electorate had rejected calls for a fundamental change in foreign policy and had voted instead in favour of Hans-Dietrich Genscher remaining as foreign-minister to pursue his 'second phase of detente'.

Coalition negotiations to decide upon a new cabinet team and common policy programme commenced between representatives of the CDU, CSU and FDP immediately the election was over. During these talks, intense bickering and back-stabbing rapidly developed between CDU and CSU leaders over who was to blame for their recent loss in national support and although Franz-Josef Strauss ruefully accepted Hans-Dietrich Genscher's re-appointment as foreign minister, he made clear his party's continued opposition to Genscher's policy approach and warned that if necessary the

[1] In the Green Party women not only form a high proportion of its elected deputies but also hold many of the key executive and policy making posts. For example, two of the most prominent, powerful and popular figures on the Greens' national executive committee, Petra Kelly and Jutta Ditfurth, are women, while four of its new six-member Bundestag leadership (including Fraktion leader Hannegret Hönes) are also female.

CSU might 'drop out (from the coalition) and only tolerate a CDU-FDP government'.[1] In the more general coalition negotiations, however, following its advances in January 1987, it was the balance-holding FDP which held the upper hand and which clearly stamped its identity over the final agreed programme. Firstly, it forced significant modifications in and liberalisation of the proposed new CSU-inspired laws for fighting terrorism and curbing violent demonstrations. Secondly, it gained a further cabinet portfolio, that of education (see Table 12), from the CDU.[2] Thirdly, and most importantly, the FDP succeeded, after three weeks of intense bargaining, in adding to the new legislative programme a radical new DM 44 billion tax reform package designed at reducing the top rate of income tax from 56% to 53%, cutting corporation tax from 56% to 50% and lowering the bottom level of income tax from 22% to 19%.

The changes to the interior ministry's proposed reforms were bitterly opposed by the CSU, while the plan to reduce taxation on higher income earners was strongly criticised by the CDU's trade unionist and blue-collar wing led by labour minister Norbert Blüm and party general-secretary Heiner Geissler. Thus, when the coalition programme was finally presented to the Bundestag on 11 March 1987, sixteen members of the ruling coalition failed to vote in favour of the Chancellor, who received a total of 253 secret-ballot Bundestag votes, only four more than the minimum number required. This, following the decline in CDU support in January 1987, represented a further blow to the diminished prestige of Chancellor Kohl and suggested that the coalition would experience an uncomfortable and unpredictable second term in office.

**Table 12 The Kohl Administration Cabinet of March 1987**

| | | |
|---|---|---|
| Dr Helmut Kohl | CDU | Federal Chancellor |
| Hans-Dietrich Genscher | FDP | Vice-Chancellor & Foreign Affairs |

(cont. p76.)

[1]Strauss, during the coalition negotiations, was offered by Kohl the choice of the finance, interior or defence ministries along with the rank of deputy-chancellor but declined them, deciding to concentrate on his work as minister-president of Bavaria.

[2]One of the party's leading figures, Dr Otto Lambsdorff (60), may also later be brought back into the cabinet after being finally cleared by the Bonn court of the charge of accepting bribes from the Flick corporation on 16 February 1987. Lambsdorff was, however, fined DM 180 000 (£67 000) for tax evasion on gifts he had accepted on behalf of the FDP. Hans Friderichs was fined DM 61 500 (£23 000) and Eberhard von Brauchitsch given a two-year suspended prison sentence and fined DM 550 000 (£204 000) for similar tax evasion.

*Table 12 – cont.*

| | | |
|---|---|---|
| Dr Manfred Wörner | CDU | Defence |
| Dr Martin Bangemann | FDP | Economic Affairs |
| Dr Gerhard Stoltenberg | CDU | Finance |
| Dr Friedrich Zimmermann | CSU | Interior |
| Wolfgang Schäuble | CDU | Head of the Chancellery |
| Hans Engelhard | FDP | Justice |
| Norbert Blüm | CDU | Labour & Social Affairs |
| Ignaz Kiechle | CSU | Agriculture |
| Jürgen Möllemann | FDP | Education |
| Walter Wallmann | CDU | Environment |
| Frau Dr Dorothee Wilms | CDU | Inner-German Affairs |
| Dr Jürgen Warnke | CSU | Transport |
| Hans Klein | CSU | Economic Co-operation |
| Dr Christian-Schwarz Schilling | CDU | Posts & Telecommunications |
| Dr Heinz Riesenhuber | CDU | Research & Technology |
| Frau Dr Rita Süssmuth | CDU | Youth, Family & Health Affairs |
| Dr Oscar Schneider | CSU | Regional Planning, Construction & Urban Development |

## Whither the opposition?: Prospects for the SPD and Greens

However, while January 1987 produced acrimony within the ruling coalition as its members fought amongst themselves over the spoils of office, for the SPD it represented a depressing realisation that former Fraktion leader Herbert Wehner's prediction in October 1982 that the party, once out of power, would face more than a decade in the wilderness before the next Machtwechsel appeared increasingly prophetic and realistic. Wehner had believed that the SPD would need to maintain itself as a moderate, respectable, 'seriös' opposition party within the Bundestag during these wilderness years, making itself ready to accommodate the FDP once the latter 'hinge party' decided to switch coalition partners once again. The dramatic rise in support for the Greens on the SPD's left flank since Wehner's 1982 prognosis had served, however, to significantly change the calculations of senior party strategists and to open up a major intra-party debate over the correct route forwards during the months following January 1987.

The lead in this debate was taken by party leftwingers, a group which during the 1986-7 campaign had been privately critical of the Rau 'centrist majority' strategy and thus had failed to give the SPD's chancellor-candidate wholehearted support. Within hours of the announcement of the federal result, Oskar Lafontaine made public, in a national press-conference, his view that Rau's ruling-out of the possibility of a 'red-green' coalition after the 1987 election had been a 'fatal mistake'. This view was echoed by fellow leftwingers at the SPD executive's post-election conclave at Bonn on 26 January 1987. The position of the left was further strengthened at this meeting when the weary and demoralised Johannes Rau announced his intention to return to North-Rhine-Westphalia and concentrate on his job as minister-president. He stated that he would remain as federal party deputy chairman, but had no desire in the future to seek the nomination as party chairman when Willy Brandt retired. Brandt had, during 1986, declared his intention of stepping down as party chairman when the next leadership elections took place in 1988. In fact, however, Brandt's tenure lasted barely two months after the January 1987 election before he was forced to prematurely resign on 23 March 1987, following mounting criticism of many of his leadership decisions and, in particular, his appointment of a young, inexperienced Greek woman with CDU-leanings. Margarita Mathiopoulos (31), as the party's new national spokesperson.[1]

The retirement of Brandt and departure of Rau from the federal stage left the door open for a new generation of younger and more radical politicians to capture control of the SPD executive machinery. The left did not succeed in immediately capturing the party chairmanship, instead the centrist Hans-Jöchen Vogel (61) was appointed to replace Brandt in March 1987. However, their leading star and the party's most dynamic and controversial politician, Oskar Lafontaine (43), popularly nicknamed the 'Ayatollah of the Saarland', did replace Vogel as party deputy chairman and thus heir-apparent during the March 1987 re-shuffle. Lafontaine's elevation to second position within the SPD was a reflection of the continuing leftward shift that had taken place with the party's ranks since the later 1970s. At the August 1986 Nuremberg conference, for example, political commentators noted that an 80% majority existed among the 780 delegates present for centre-left policy positions, while, almost without exception, all the new members elected to the SPD's 42-member national executive

[1]Mathiopoulos, despite impressive academic qualifications, was criticised for not being a member of the SPD and as having previously applied for a post under the CDU minister Heinz Riesenhuber and for currently being engaged to marry a CDU member. She resigned from her post along with Brandt in March 1987.

were drawn from what has been termed the 'new left'.[1] Faced with a further four years in opposition, the SPD's leftward drift, which is particularly evident on defence and environmental issues rather than in the economic sphere, seems set to continue and calls for the sanctioning of coalitions with the Greens at the Länder level will, in the future, be more favourably supported by the central party apparatus.

The 'red-green' strategy propounded by the SPD's rising stars Lafontaine and Engholm entails the danger, however, of alienating substantial support from moderate 'Schmidtite voters', thus further boosting the state and national rating of the FDP. It also encounters the considerable problem presented by the unpredictability and unreliability of the Greens as coalition partners. This was made clear to the SPD's central leaders in February 1987 when the fourteen month old SPD-Greens Land Coalition government in Hesse suddenly collapsed after the Greens' environment minister, Joschka Fischer, tendered his resignation on 9 February following SPD minister-president Holger Börner's refusal to sanction the closure of a local plutonium factory.[2] Fischer's decision to resign was reflective of a hardening in attitude among the Greens towards the terms they would demand for entering coalition governments. The party had increased in confidence following its advances in January 1987 and its 'Fundi' wing was in the ascendant. This was reflected by the election of the radical Hamburg 'eco-socialist', Thomas Ebermann (35), in place of the 'Realo' Otto Schily as one of the Greens' six Bundestag executive committee members, and by the declaration in February 1987 by national leader Rainer Trampert that the party would not rush into coalition pacts but would wait until the SPD had more thoroughly 'renewed themselves', adding 'We are sitting firmly in the saddle'. Faced with such obstacles in the way of a durable 'red-green' alliance and with the existence of a clear conservative majority within the country in favour of a freer-market and more individualist economic strategy

[1]The term 'new left' has been used to denote a new group of, usually university-educated, white-collar professionals within the party who have adopted a radical stance on the 'post-materialist' issues of nuclear power, the environment and defence and who support an individualist and libertarian approach to economic and social issues. They differ markedly in both background and outlook from the blue-collar, centrist party workers of the 1960s and early 1970s who supported a firm defence policy and placed major stress on jobs and social welfare.

[2]Börner (56) immediately retired as minister-president and was replaced by Land finance minister Hans Krollmann who called fresh elections for April 1987

and a cautious and firm defence policy, the SPD's hopes of recapturing power at the federal level during the early 1990s appear remote. At the Länder level, however, the party retains a firm foothold in the northern states and has the prospect, with local Green support, to make further advances which may even put the CDU-CSU Bundesrat majority in jeopardy. These Länder bases will prove vital in maintaining party unity and credibility during the SPD's period in the federal wilderness.

## Extra-Parliamentary Activity : Extremism and Terrorism

The postwar West German state, concerned to prevent a possible recrudesence of Nazism, has been most vigilant in its efforts to curb political extremism. Radical 'anti-constitutional' parties have been banned and their members have been debarred from public service.[1] However, despite these measures there have been periodic revivals of extremist activity, particularly during periods of cyclical depression. In addition, a new problem of political terrorism emerged during the 1970s among radical far-left groups who remained critical of what they saw as the controlled oppression of the contemporary bourgeois political system and who rejected the use of the ballot box and instead concentrated on direct, de-stabilising action.

This leftwing terrorist activity peaked during the 1970s and was centred around the alienated middle class Baader-Meinhof gang. The leaders of this group were captured and imprisoned in June 1972 and eventually committed suicide in their cells in May 1976 and October 1977. However, splinter groups — for example, the Red Army Faction, the June 2nd Movement and the West Berlin and Düsseldorf-centred Revolutionary Cells — continued the spate of hi-jacks, kidnappings and murders which reached a chilling crescendo in 1977 with the triple assassinations of the federal prosecutor, Siegfried Buback (April 1977), the banker, Jurgen Ponto (July 1977), and the president of the employers' association, Hans-

---

[1] Recently, however, there have been signs of a wish to relax these *Berufsverbot* (professional ban) job-vetting rules (which were originally introduced in January 1972), with the new Saarland government, for example, having ended the political vetting of public employees and West German courts proving less willing to uphold dismissals on political grounds.

Martin Schleyer (October 1977), and the hijacking of a Lufthansa airliner at Mogadishu (October 1977). During the following five years terrorist activities subsided both as a result of the successful efforts of the police and newly established GSG−9 (*Grenzschutzgruppe 9*) anti-terrorist unit in capturing a large proportion of the most wanted terrorists and as a result of a diversion of potential new recruits into alternative channels — for example, into the peaceful Green movement. However, between 1983 and 1987 terrorism began to revive once more, though at a reduced level compared to the mid-1970s. American and NATO military officials, rather than politicians or industrialists, became the new targets for kidnappings and bomb threats in these new campaigns which were sometimes carried out in collaboration with the French terrorist organisation *Action Directe*, the Italian *Red Brigades* and varied Arab-based groups. These incidents moved towards another peak in 1985-7 with the assassinations of the arms-industry executive, Ernst Zimmermann (February 1985), Siemens executive Karl-Heinz Beckurts (July 1986), and the senior civil servant, Gerold von Braunmuhl (October 1986), and the destructive bombings of the US Rhine-Main air base (August 1985) and West Berlin American disco (April 1986). Inside the prisons, captured terrorists also engaged in periodic hunger strikes in an attempt to gain preferential conditions.

Outside these narrow terrorist cells, a broader based and non-violent protest movement emerged on the left and among the young during the 1980s in the form of the huge, anti-nuclear, peace and environmental demonstrations which were organised by the new Green Party. More violent were the squatter riots which erupted in West Berlin and Nuremberg during the spring of 1981 and the anti-police disturbances in Frankfurt in September 1985, which followed the death of Günter Sare (36), who had been knocked over by a water canon vehicle during a protest against an NPD neo-Nazi party meeting. Terrorist, anarchist (*Autonomen*) and extremist factions attempted to attach themselves to the fringes of these movements, becoming most prominent in the violent anti-nuclear demonstrations of June 1986.

The leftwing terrorist organisations remained, however, insignificant in terms of the numbers involved — the revived Red Army Faction possessing only 25 hard-core activists in 1986 and an estimated 2000 'sympathisers'. It was rightwing extremist organisations which presented the greater danger during the early 1980s. These groups thrived during economic recessions, as the brief rise of the NPD between 1966 and 1969 had previously demonstrated. [1] The years between 1980 and 1985 were the most depressed since the inter-war period, with unemployment rising to more than two million and with the issue of *Gastarbeiter* (foreign workers) producing a xenophobia which could be manipulated by the extreme right. There was thus a small revival in the activities of neo-fascist groups during these years — the most striking of which was their planting of a bomb at the Munich beer festival on 26 September 1980, killing thirteen people and injuring more than two hundred. However, the far right remained disorganised — there existing in 1981 more than 83 neo-fascist groups with a combined membership of 20 000 and twenty-two fanatical 'action groups' with less than one thousand members. The largest single organisation was the NPD with a membership of 15 000. The NPD failed however to make significant advances in the federal elections of October 1980 and March 1983, capturing barely 0.2% of the national vote. (This represented support from only 70 000-90 000 voters in total). The tough immigration stance adopted by the Kohl administration and, in particular by interior minister Friedrich Zimmermann, helped, to some extent, to take the sting out of such right wing extremism between 1982-5. Only in 1986-7, with the emergence of the newly formed far-right Republican Party[2] in Bavaria, which captured 3% of the vote in the Land election of October 1986, and with the tripling in support (to 0.6%) for the NPD in the Bundestag election of January 1987, did the extremist parties show signs of gaining ground.

In general, however, support for extremism remained remarkably

[1] The NPD (*Nationaldemokratische Partei Deutschlands* — National Democratic Party) had been formed in November 1964 out of a merger of the DRP (*Deutsche Reichs-Partei*) and GDP (*Gesamtdeutsche Partei*). Between November 1966 and April 1968 it gained representation in the majority of Länder, capturing 9.8% of the vote in Baden-Württemberg, and enjoyed considerable support from lower-middle class groups, small towns and rural areas during a period when agriculture was depressed and there was considerable public alienation and antipathy towards the newly formed 'Grand Coalition'. The party's vote fell, however, to 4.3% in the September 1969 federal election and, since it failed to enter the Bundestag, its support rapidly drained away to the CDU and CSU during the 1970s. In September 1972 the NPD captured only 0.6% of the national vote and by this date the 'flash party' had lost representation in all the Landtage.

[2] The Republican Party, which included former CSU deputies (see page 50) was, by 1986, led by Franz Schonhüber, a former Nazi Waffen-SS officer, and boasted a membership of 4000 (80% of whom were in Bavaria). It opposed trade unions, membership of the EEC and sought to repatriate immigrants.

limited during the troubled early 1980s. It was rather the more pacific radical groups — the Greens and anti-nuclear organisations — which attracted support and which were tolerated by the political authorities. This was an indication of the growing political maturity of the West German political system. It also, however, reflected the capacity of the West German economy to cope more successfully than neighbouring countries with the difficulties presented by the economic changes of this period.

# Part Three

# ECONOMIC AND SOCIAL DEVELOPMENTS: 1976–1987

## The West German Economy to 1974 — the 'Miracle Years'

In 1946 the West German economy lay in ruins. Its cities and factories had been bombed and destroyed and half its eastern territory had been lost to Poland and the GDR. Yet less than three decades later West Germany's industrial base had been fully rebuilt. The Federal Republic now ranked as the third major western market economy (behind the US and Japan) and its citizens enjoyed a per capita income which was exceeded only by the United States, Scandinavia, Switzerland and the oil rich principalities of the Middle East. The postwar regeneration of West Germany has been so dramatic that the period between 1948 and 1974 has been termed one of 'economic miracle' (*Wirtschaftswunder*).

This economic recovery was achieved through hard, responsible labour by its educated and expanding population and through high levels of industrial investment. The inflow of Marshall aid and a high domestic saving ratio provided the funds: refugees from the dismembered eastern sector and later workers from the Mediterranean lands and from agriculture provided the hands to man the new factories at competitive wage levels. These factories were equipped with up-to-date machinery and geared towards the expanding markets of postwar Europe — machine tools, electrical goods, steel, automobiles, consumer durables and chemicals. Growth was export-led, with the European Community providing a wide integrated market on Germany's doorstep and with the Korean war boosting demand during the 1950s. Germany has thus become heavily dependent on foreign trade, with manufactured goods' exports today accounting for 30% of its GNP (Gross National Product) and with large amounts of raw materials, energy products and foodstuffs flowing inwards to feed and fuel the expanding economy.

The CDU-FDP government presided over the German economy during the 'miracle years', providing a stable monetary and fiscal framework within which private companies could flourish while encouraging responsible co-operation from the trade union movement. From the mid-1960s state intervention in the economy, both direct and indirect, increased. In 1963 a five man panel of economists, the Council of Experts, was established to report to the government each year on economic trends and between 1966 and 1969 the SPD's economic expert, Karl Schiller, dabbled with Keynesian fiscal stimuli to pull Germany out of the contemporary recession. In 1967 the role of government in steering and managing the economy was most clearly set out in the Stability and Growth Act. This called upon the government to seek to maintain a stable price level, full employment and a foreign trade equilibrium, fine-tuning the economy when necessary through the use of fiscal indicators.

Under the succeeding SPD-FDP administrations of Willy Brandt and Helmut Schmidt government intervention increased, as a unique corporalist form of economic management was developed in West Germany. To achieve improved control over government spending, medium term financial planning was now introduced, and to achieve closer co-ordination between federal and state policies and expenditure two bodies, the Financial Planning Council (*Finanzplanungsrat*) and the Counter-Cyclical Advisory Council (*Konjunkturrat*), were now established. The third innovation introduced by the SPD-FDP administration was the establishment of annual Concerted Action (*Konzertierte Aktion*) meetings which brought together leading figures from within industry, banking, the trade unions and government to discuss general economic conditions and to agree upon guidelines for government spending, taxation and wage and price rises in the private sector. Under Helmut Schmidt, who maintained close personal relationships with prominent financiers and industrialists, this expert corporatist approach was taken furthest. Throughout this period government's direct involvement in the economy also increased as, with rising social and welfare spending, the state's share of GNP rose from 38% in 1969 to a peak of 51% in 1981, with 25% of the workforce now being employed in the public sector.

The growth performance of the West German postwar economy has been impressive, as has been the maturity of its interest group participants. Nevertheless the rate of economic growth, as in other Western economies, has decelerated during recent decades. West German GNP, which increased at a rate of more than 6% per capita during the 1950s, and by 4% per capita during the 1960s, grew by barely 2.3% during the 1970s. This rate is still impressive compared to that registered by Britain or the United States, but it is well behind that recorded by Japan. The German locomotive has clearly been running out of steam, particularly since the mid-1970s.

The quadrupling of world oil prices which followed both the Arab-Israeli war of 1973 and the Iranian revolution of 1979 was one important factor behind Germany's recent sluggish economic performance. These oil hikes were a turning point in West Germany's postwar economic history — making the end of more than two decades of unparalleled economic growth fuelled by cheap, abundant oil and by expanding world trade, declining tariff barriers and stable exchange rates. They inaugurated an era of stagnant international trade, volatile exchange rate movements, incipient protectionism and structural transformation, as the mature German economy adjusted to the three challenges of more expensive fuel, new technologies and increased competition from the 'Newly Industrialised Countries' (NICs) of South-East Asia and ascendant Japan.

In this section the economic fortunes of the German economy between 1974 and 1987 are first briefly sketched, before a number of the important broader trends are examined. At the close of this section the actions of politicians, employers and trade unions during these troubled years are examined, with an analysis of policy prescriptions and repercussions.

## The German Economy: 1974-1987

The 1973-4 oil price hike chipped away roughly 2% from West Germany's national income and precipitated a sharp recession between 1973 and 1975, before the economy learned to adjust to the changed circumstances of the post-OPEC world. The level of unemployment in West Germany shot up from barely a quarter of a million at the start of the 1970s to more than one million (4% of the working population) in 1974, inflation rose to a peak of 7% and the public-sector deficit increased from 0.7% of GNP in 1973 to 5.4% in 1975. Such was the severity of this short recession that West Germany's GNP actually declined by 2.5% in 1974. The country recovered quickly, however, aided at first by a budgetary and investment stimulus in 1975, before it set about quadrupling its exports of manufactured goods — machinery and consumer items — to the oil rich economies of the Middle East, thus restoring its trading balance with this region.

Recovery was clearly evident by 1977. Unemployment had fallen below the psychological barrier of one million, the public-sector deficit had been trimmed to 2.7% of GNP and inflation was kept down to below 3%. Economic growth was particularly sharp in 1975, with GNP increasing by 5.8%, before settling at 2% per annum during the following two years as the government maintained a careful budgetary stance. By 1978, however, there were fears that the German recovery might stall — being choked at home by a tightening fiscal stance and by a spate of industrial disputes and being threatened abroad by vanishing markets and growing protectionism. In such circumstances, Chancellor Schmidt decided at the Bonn summit of June 1978 to risk large-scale reflation to the tune of DM 13 billion (equivalent to 1% of GNP) through the extension of tax concessions to industry and to consumers. The German economy, which had been criticised during the early 1970s for maintaining a huge overseas trading surplus of more than $10 billion per annum, was now to act as the 'locomotive' to pull the world economy out of a threatened new recession. This reflation proved to be a startling short-term success, with West Germany's GNP increasing by 3.5% and 4% in 1978 and 1979, at the cost though of an increase in the inflation rate and growth in the budget deficit. It was a rare example of a home-demand, rather than export, based recovery in West Germany.

However, although the West German economy fared better than most of its European competitors during the 1970s, there were, by 1980, signs of a longer term decline in competitiveness, particularly vis-a-vis the NICs of South-East Asia and the thrusting power of Japan. One important factor behind this relative decline had been the rise in German labour costs during recent years and the decline in the country's traditional passion for hard and extensive labour, evidenced by opinion poll data and by the extension in holiday periods and the shortening of the working week. By 1979 West Germany's labour costs per hour (including social security charges) amounted to DM 21 compared to a figure of DM 12 in Japan. Productivity increases had in the past paid for such wage increases, but by the 1970s Germany was faced with fierce Far Eastern competitors devoted to the work ethic to an even greater degree, and which enjoyed lower average labour costs and rising rates of productivity. A second factor behind Germany's competitive problems was the upvaluation of the traditionally undervalued Deutsche Mark which followed the establishment of, first, floating exchange rates in 1973 and, then, the European Monetary System (EMS) in 1979. A third factor, which has been common to other West European nations, was the increasing level of government welfare spending between 1966 and 1980. This had begun to 'crowd out' private investment and had placed increased burdens on employers in terms of insurance contributions. In such circumstances, and with profits being squeezed at home, the growth rate for domestic German industrial investment began to decline during the 1970s, while German investment abroad, particularly in the United States but also in developing nations, increased dramatically.

Matters came to a head between 1980 and 1985 with the second oil crisis and the slump in world trade. The German economy was plunged into its deepest recession since the inter-war period. In 1979, as a result of the sudden rise in the cost of the country's oil import bill, West Germany recorded its first trade deficit since 1965. This was followed by a sharp rise in the unemploymnent level, breaching the one million barrier in 1981 before climbing to an average of 2.3 million in the years between 1983 and 1985 (a rate equivalent to 9% of the working population — see Table 13). Inflation also edged upwards towards 5%, while interest rates moved up even higher. The severity of this recession was reflected by the fact that Germany's GNP actually declined in two successive years between 1981 and 1982 and grew by only 1% in 1983. With stagnant world markets, Germany found it impossible, before 1984, to export its way out of recession as had occurred between 1976 and 1979. It was not helped in this respect by the political and economic collapse during these years of a number of important new markets for German goods, for example, the debt-ridden states of Eastern Europe, and the troubled oil states of Nigeria, Iran and her Middle Eastern neighbours — countries which had taken almost 17% of West Germany's total exports in 1977. To make matters worse, competition also now intensified, both at home and abroad, from Japan and the NICs in a number of West Germany's traditional lines — for example, automobiles, machine tools and electrical goods. West Germany's traditional industries bore the brunt of the recession and the country was slow in pushing forward with the new 'high-tech' industries of the 1980s which were making headway in the United States and Japan.

Table 13   West German Economic Indicators, 1977-1986

|  | 1977 | 1978 | 1979 | 1980 | 1981 | 1982 | 1983 | 1984 | 1985 | 1986 |
|---|---|---|---|---|---|---|---|---|---|---|
| Industrial Prod. | +2.0% | +3.5% | +3.5% | −5.0% | 0.0% | −5.5% | +1.9% | +4.6% | +3.8% | +1.3% |
| Inflation | 4.0% | 2.0% | 5.5% | 5.5% | 6.5% | 4.5% | 2.6% | 2.1% | 1.8% | 1.0% |
| Wage Rises | 6.0% | 5.5% | 5.0% | 7.5% | 5.0% | 4.0% | 3.1% | 3.1% | 1.9% | 4.1% |
| MS Growth | 10.0% | 13.5% | 5.5% | 3.5% | −2.0% | 6.5% | 6.5% | 2.2% | 4.4% | 6.8% |
| Unemployment | 4.6% | 4.2% | 3.6% | 4.1% | 6.5% | 8.5% | 9.2% | 9.1% | 9.1% | 8.7% |
| Trade Balance | +16bn | +20bn | +15bn | +6bn | +10bn | +21bn | +18bn | +17bn | +24bn | +50bn |
| DM Exchange Rate (per dollar) | 2.2 | 1.8 | 1.7 | 1.9 | 2.3 | 2.4 | 2.7 | 3.1 | 2.5 | 1.8 |

87

The spread of protectionism throughout the world economy and the adoption of unusually rigid fiscal policies by the CDU-CSU-FDP administration to maintain control over inflation and the budget deficit served to further exacerbate the situation during this transitional period. In such circumstances, recovery from the 1980-3 recession has been slow when compared to that from the troughs of 1966 and 1974, with unemployment continuing to rise as technological innovation economised on labour inputs in both the manufacturing and clerical sectors. From 1984, however, strong pump-primed demand in the United States coupled with a decline in the value of the Deutsche Mark gave an export boost to the West German economy. The country's rationalised and newly efficient firms made full use of this opportunity and exports boomed in 1984 and 1985, providing the basis for overall GNP growth of 2.6% and 2.4% respectively. This growth gained momentum and became more evenly balanced in 1986 as the sharp fall in OPEC oil prices gave a boost to world trade and as German home demand was stimulated by tax cuts and rising real incomes. Real GNP growth of 3.5% was thus registered in 1986 and unemployment began to fall from a peak of 2.5 million at a rate of more than 200 000 per annum.

By the autumn of 1986 the German economy was thus in its healthiest condition for more than a decade. The inflation rate averaged barely 1.5% and reached negative figures during a number of months in 1986. The budget deficit, which had stood at 4.1% of GNP in 1982, had been reduced to only 1.5% (one of the lowest levels in the industrialised world), overall public expenditure had been trimmed to 47.5% of GNP and interest rates had correspondingly fallen to only 8.5%. Industrial output, investment and productivity were booming and record trade surpluses were being recorded, as the country's new computer and office automation industries began to make their mark on world markets. The only adverse statistic for the CDU-CSU-FDP government was that for unemployment, which still exceeded 2.2 million.

This unemployment was largely structural in nature, being caused by technological change and demographic factors. The Kohl administration was, however, charged by the SPD opposition with exacerbating matters through its unduly rigid and doctrinaire fiscal stance. In addition, its economic strategy was viewed as socially divisive, unduly benefiting the rich and privileged at the expense of the poor, and, with the existence of more than 700 000 long-term unemployed unable to claim full social benefits, the government was seen as creating a 'new poverty' within the once affluent postwar German state. Overseas, competitor governments in Europe and America also criticised the Kohl administration's tight fiscal stance. They felt that Germany, along with Japan, should pursue a more active role in helping to reflate the world economy and should reduce their huge current-account surplus. Recognising these criticisms, the Kohl government made some small adjustments to its policy approach after 1985. It assented to a two-staged DM 20 billion package of tax cuts to be introduced in 1986 and 1988, introduced a series of new re-training schemes and slightly loosened its monetary and budgetary corset. These measures were viewed as too limited by independent economic research institutes in West Germany, Europe and America, but the Kohl government remained determined to pursue a solid and steady growth path rather than risk a repeat of the 1978−9 abortive 'dash for growth'.

## Trends in the Contemporary West German Economy and Society

### Energy policy in the OPEC era

For energy-deficient West Germany the rise in world oil prices from $2 a barrel in the early 1970s to $38 in 1981 was of particular consequence. The country's only indigenous natural sources of fuel were coal and hydro-electricity. Two-thirds of its energy require-ments were therefore imported — 50% being supplied by oil, 10% by gas — with key sectors, for example the large West German chemical industry, being unusually dependent upon Middle Eastern suppliers. During the nine years between 1973 and 1981, as a result of the OPEC measures, the country found its fuel costs increasing by 192%. The German government was thus faced with an immediate problem of paying for its vital oil imports and with the longer term need to lessen its dependence upon imported oil.

The first difficulty was overcome between 1973 and 1979 by a spectacular expansion of West German manufactured exports to the Middle Eastern oil states. This, however, proved impossible to repeat between 1980 and 1985. The longer-term problem of changing Germany's energy balance has proved to be even more intractable and has fuelled a significant political debate.

The German government's energy programme between 1974-86 concentrated upon four areas — the encouragement of energy conservation, the revival of the declining coal industry, the expansion of the nuclear energy programme, and the importation of natural gas from Eastern Europe. Most success was gained in energy conservation and in gas diversification.

The West German coal industry had been in decline since the 1950s, with its manpower falling from almost 400 000 to under 200 000 by the later 1970s. Workers in the industry had retired or had been transferred to new expanding industries during the 'miracle years'. The industry still, however, remained substantial (the second largest in the West, producing 226 million tonnes per annum, its output only being exceeded by the United States) and relatively efficient, and it possessed reserves equivalent to more than 200 years' consumption. The government's enthusiasm for the coal industry was rekindled by the oil scare of 1973−4. Plans were now made, in common with other Western governments, to introduce new technology and to expand gross output, and experiments were entered into by the Rheinbraun group to examine the possibility of converting brown coal into synthetic petrol and fuel. Government subsidies paid to the coal industry were now raised and the electricity industry was now compelled to burn indigenous coal.

Plans were also made during the mid-1970s to press forward with West Germany's nuclear energy programme. Included in this programme was the introduction of the controversial fast breeder reactor. This programme envisaged the construction of more than fifteen new nuclear power stations, with the ultimate goal of producing 75 000 MW of electricity (56% of projected power needs) by the end of the century from sixty stations. Chancellor Schmidt was a committed supporter of this programme, viewing nuclear power as a vital transitional 'bridge' which energy-deficient West Germany must draw upon before new alternative energy sources could later be substituted. In addition, the expansion of nuclear energy output was seen by Helmut Schmidt as crucial in lessening the country's dangerous dependence upon energy drawn from the unpredictable Middle East region.

The introduction of this extensive nuclear power programme brought, however, great opposition from the left wings of both the SPD and FDP and from the new Green movement. It proved difficult to implement, with projects being held up by court appeals, huge demonstrations and by worried state governments. Thus by 1980 only fourteen nuclear power stations were in operation in West Germany — producing 9000 MW and providing a mere 3.3% of the nation's primary energy requirements and 14.5% of its electricity needs. Nine more stations were in the process of construction and a further two were held up in the courts. In the years between 1977 and 1981 only one new German reactor came into service. In contrast, in neighbouring France, where environmentalist opposition was more muted, the number of operational nuclear power stations increased from twelve to thirty during the corresponding period, providing almost 38% of the country's electricity needs. The second oil price hike of 1979-80 gave increased urgency to the nuclear programme, which the new Kohl administration backed vigorously, but public opposition continued to prevent expansion at a more than crab-like rate. By 1986 Germany boasted 19 operating reactors supplying 30% of electricity needs, with a new reactor at Brokdorf and a reprocessing plant at Wackersdorf due to come on stream.[1] The April 1986 Chernobyl accident in the Soviet Union further increased public opposition to any further expansion of the nuclear programme, but the Kohl administration remained firm, convinced as it was of the vital importance of nuclear power in maintaining West Germany's economic pre-eminence.

The coal industry expansion programme similarly ran into opposition from environmentalists during the early 1980s, when it was discovered that the sulphur dioxide emissions from coal-fired power stations were creating acid rain which was destroying the fir forests of southern Germany at an alarming rate. (By 1986 50% of West Germany's forests and 80% of its fir trees were affected by this poisoning). The government was forced to take action, and in February 1983 legislation was passed which required large power stations to fit filters and smaller stations to cut sulphur dioxide emissions sixfold within a decade. Even before this date, however, enthusiasm for the expansion of the coal industry had begun to wane as demand for fuel had failed to rise as had been projected. The deepening industrial recession and structural changes in the economy had led to a fall in demand from the traditional coal burning industries, particularly steel, and this deficit had not been bridged by increased demand from the new 'sunrise' industries, which were low consumers of energy per value of output. In addition, substantial economies were being made during these years in domestic and industrial energy consumption — stimulated

[1]In France, by contrast, 40 nuclear reactors were in operation in 1986 supplying 65% of the country's electricity requirements.

by the Schmidt administration's energy conservation packages of 1977 and 1979 — as conservation became a significant third plank in the country's energy programme. This conservation programme spawned a small industrial sector of its own, which attracted both small scale entrepreneurs and even traditional heavy industry giants such as the Mannesmann corporation.

The fourth element of the West German energy programme has been the expansion of natural gas consumption and the diversification in its sources of supply. The German North Sea sector has proven, thus far, to be almost barren in gas or oil riches, but a long pipeline was established at Emden (Lower Saxony) by Ruhr-Gas to tap the large Norwegian Eldfisk field. This augmented existing supplies from the Dutch Groningen field. This was followed in 1982 by the signing of a major $15 billion pipeline deal between a Franco-German consortium and the Soviet government. The European consortium agreed to supply pipeline equipment on credit in return for a Russian undertaking to supply gas from its huge Urengoy field in Siberia without charge for 10 years and thereafter at an agreed rate. This 3000 mile pipeline, which will be opened after 1986, is intended to supply 30% of West German gas requirements by 1990. Diversification in oil supply, away from the unstable Middle East, was also achieved during the early 1980s through importations from the British and Norwegian North Sea fields: by 1982 Britain had overtaken Saudi Arabia as West Germany's largest single oil supplier.

The period between 1974 and 1987 was thus one of considerable restructuring and change for German energy consumption and supply. Total energy consumption rose by only 1.4% per annum between 1974−82 compared to a rise of 4.4% per annum between 1960−74. This former figure was well below the rate of industrial growth (2% per annum) and outlined the advances that had been made in fuel efficiency and consumption. Changes in the mix of energy types consumed were not as marked as had once been anticipated — oil remaining the major fuel — but supply sources had become more diversified and the share taken by coal, nuclear power and gas had increased significantly. West Germany's energy base in 1987 was thus broader and more evenly balanced. The country still, however, remained overwhelmingly dependent upon external suppliers.

## Population movements and their consequences

West Germany's population expanded from only 42 million in

1946 to 55.4 million in 1960, and continued to rise to a peak of 62.1 million in 1973. Such growth was caused at first by a rising birthrate during the 1950s 'miracle years' and by the influx of more than 10 million refugees from the divided east. It was boosted during the 1960s by the immigration of 2.6 million temporary foreign 'guest workers' (Gastarbeiter) from the Mediterranean region — Turkey, Yugoslavia, Italy, Greece and Spain — working in the coal mines, car factories, chemical works and public services, filling unpopular menial posts at low wages.

West Germany's population structure as it entered the 1970s was thus young (36% of the total being under the age of 25) and heterogenous — being composed of a mixture of refugess (22%), Gastarbeiter (4%), Catholics (45%) and Protestants (47%). During the preceding two decades there had been major changes in occupation and outlook, with the decline in the proportion of the workforce engaged in agriculture (forming 23% of the total in 1950: only 5% in 1980), a rise in the white-collar service sector (employing 21% in 1950: 45% in 1980), and a growth in secularism, as church attendance became less popular.

During the decade of stagnant growth and recession which followed the oil shock of 1973−4 there was an acceleration in the speed of change — particularly in the movement towards the service sector and the structural decline of traditional industries. There was also, however, an attempt to check and reverse the inflow of foreign Gastarbeiter as racial tensions mounted during this period of rising unemployment.

*The Immigration Question.* By 1973 2.6 million Gastarbeiter resided and worked in West Germany. During the 1960s and early 1970s they had been accepted as essential cogs in the successfully functioning German economy. However, with the onset of recession after 1973, they bore the brunt of criticism for the rising level of unemployment. Action was thus taken to halt the further inflow of Gastarbeiter in 1973, when a ban was imposed upon the recruitment of workers from outside the EEC. This achieved its immediate goal — by 1984 the number of Gastarbeiter had been reduced to only 1.9 million. Immigrant workers continued, however, to enter West Germany by less direct routes.

The first and most direct channel of entry involved the wives and children of resident foreign workers who were allowed to join their husbands. They established new families with birth rates well above

93

the German average and thus boosted the size of the immigrant community from within. The second channel of entry was less direct. It took the form of refugees entering Germany in search of 'political asylum'. They were encouraged by West Germany's liberal entry laws which allowed refugees to remain in the country, work and claim welfare benefits while their cases were being dealt with by the courts — this could take, with appeals, up to four years. The number of such 'refugees' increased between 1972 and 1980 from 5300 per annum to 108 000. Less than 10% of these claims were eventually accepted, but thousands of other 'economic refugees' gained temporary residence before final deportation. A third channel of entry was from Eastern Europe, particularly from Poland during the crisis years between 1979 and 1982 when more than 100 000 were accepted into West Germany. The fourth channel remained always open — through the EEC, for Italian and later Greek workers.

Through such direct and indirect means, the number of foreigners resident in West Germany continued to increase between 1974 and 1984 — rising from 4 million to 4.7 million (representing 7.6% of the total population). Popular antipathy to the immigrant community increased during this period, as immigrant workers took the blame for Germany's economic difficulties — even though unemployment rates were in fact far higher among the often unskilled and ill-educated sons and daughters of immigrant families. (In 1983 350 000 of the two million unemployed were drawn from the immigrant community). The large poorly integrated Turkish community — which totalled 1.7 million in 1984 — with its distinctive Islamic lifestyle and its concentration in inner city ghettoes in West Berlin, Düsseldorf and Hamburg, bore the brunt of this hostility. Immigrants from Poland and Eastern Europe were more warmly accepted.

The SPD-FDP administration of Helmut Schmidt and Interior Minister Gerhart Baum (FDP) decided to take action to check infringements of the immigration rules in December 1980 by tightening up the regulations for political asylum. Under a new bill which was now introduced, would-be refugees needed to first obtain a visa before gaining entry to West Germany. During their first year of stay work permits would no longer be issued, welfare benefits would be paid in kind not cash, and the vetting and litigation procedures would be speeded up so that cases would be decided in months not years. These new regulations had immediate results — the number of applications for political asylum falling by more than 50% to only 49 000 in 1981.[1] The Schmidt administration also tightened up the direct entry regulations in December 1980, when another bill limited the immigration of the dependents of settled Gastarbeiter and refugees to those below the age of sixteen.

During the early 1980s, as unemployment rose remorselessly above two million, public opinion hardened against the Gastarbeiter. Local citizens' action groups began to campaign for *'Ausländer raus'* ('foreigners out') and squatter riots errupted in West Berlin. This persuaded the new administration of Helmut Kohl to take firmer action to deal with the immigrant problem. The liberal-minded Gerhart Baum was thus replaced at the Interior Ministry by CSU rightwinger Friedrich Zimmermann and in November 1983 a package of measures was introduced which included monetary inducements for the voluntary repatriation of unemployed foreign workers. This measure had some success, with more than 100 000 having registered for repatriation by September 1984. An attempt was also now made by the Foreign Ministry to persuade the Turkish government to agree to an annulment of articles of the 1970 EEC 'associate membership' treaty, which, due to come into effect in 1986, would have allowed the free entry of Turkish citizens once again.

These measures by the CDU-CSU-FDP government served to place a temporary check upon the inflow of foreign workers and upon the growth rate of the immigrant community, and they assuaged political discontent during a period of economic recession. Foreign workers continued, however, to play a vital role in the functioning of key sectors of the German economy and their proportionate size and contribution promised to increase further in future years as the German birth rate continued to fall and its population stagnate.

*The Declining Birthrate.* West Germany's population peaked in 1973 at 62.1 million and has been steadily declining during the last decade. By 1980 it had reached 61.4 million, and it has been projected to fall to 58 million in 1990 and to only 39 million in the year 2030. Such population contraction has been caused by a sharp drop in the German birthrate since the late 1960s to barely 10 per 1000 people — the lowest rate in the world. The primary factor behind this decreasing birthrate was the spread of the contraceptive

---

[1] Applications for political asylum, many coming through the 'Berlin hole', rose sharply again, however, in 1985 and 1986 to a level of almost 75,000 per annum. This led to further calls for a tightening of the asylum regulations.

pill during the 1970s. It has been spurred on, however, by economic and social factors — for example, by the increased level of full-time female employment, particularly that of married women; the short hours of German schooling; the high cost and scarcity of family housing; and the increasing material orientation of society. Recent additions to state family allowance payments have done nothing to reverse this demographic trend.

West Germany's population decline promises to have serious medium-term consequences for the economy. The 'dependency ratio' (the ratio of retired persons per worker) will rise sharply from 0.46 in 1980 to 0.89 in 2030 and the cost of health services will mount as the population ages. At the same time, however, savings will be made in education, as school rolls continue to fall. These prospective changes, as in other Western European countries, have given rise to a fierce debate on the future of the welfare state and balance of public spending. Population stagnation has also presented serious problems for the West German army (*Bundeswehr*), half of whose manpower of 495 000 are young compulsory conscripts. The fall in the birth rate and rise in conscientious objection during the early 1980s 'peace years' has forced the Kohl administration to pass unpopular legislation which will lengthen the period of military service from fifteen to eighteen months after 1989.

West Germany's declining birth rate has, however, proved useful in one respect during recent years. It has prevented the kind of rise in youth unemployment during the 1980—5 recession, which has been experienced in neighbouring countries. The number of sixteen-year-olds in Germany peaked in 1980 at 1.08 million and will fall to only 630 000 in 1990. This, coupled with recruitment into the Bundeswehr and into three year vocational training apprenticeships (for 90% of sixteen-year-old school leavers), has kept youth unemployment at only 9% — a rate similar to the adult average. This has undoubtedly been a factor in calming social tensions during a difficult period. Unemployment remains a more serious problem for Germans in their early twenties unable to secure a job after the end of their training contract.

## Structural Change in the 1974—1984 Recession

West Germany entered the 1970s with a strong manufacture-centred economy built around the steel, automobile, engineering, machine tools, chemical and electrical industries. Only Hong Kong and the GDR could exceed West Germany's figure of 46% for the proportion of the workforce engaged as manual workers: the European Community average was 39%. These core industries were unusually export orientated, with more than half of production being sent to foreign markets, the most important being the EEC (which received 48% of West Germany's exports), other adjoining West European states (22%), North America (10%), Eastern Europe (6%) and the lesser developed countries (LDCs) of Africa, Asia and Latin America (13%). These industries were large and corporatist in organisation, built around a specific managerial and technological ethos. However, by the close of the 1970s these industries and this form of organisation were under dual attack from the aggressive, low cost producers from the NICs and from the small-scale 'new technology' entrepreneurs from the United States and Japan. The traditional industrial base of the West German economy, with its emphasis upon capital goods, was becoming obsolete. Major restructuring and changes in outlook and organisation were required as the 1980-4 recession bit deep. This involved both further investment at home to modernise and upgrade existing factories and the continued growth of the service sector, as well as increased investment and sub-contracting abroad in the NICs and LDCs to supply less complex inputs at low cost.

Rationalisation and re-organisation of the West German coal industry took place during the boom years of the 1950s and 1960s as the economy switched from coal to oil consumption. Miners were re-trained and re-deployed in newer industries under the umbrella of the state created Economic Development Corporation. For the West German steel industry, restructuring was more painful and delayed. In 1980 West Germany's steel industry was still the largest in Europe (accounting for 31% of EEC steel production and employing 200 000 workers) and the fifth largest in the world, being based around seven large private companies — the giant Thyssen and Krupp groups based at Duisburg and Rheinhausen in the Rhine region; Hoesch, Kloeckner and Peine-Salzgitter from the Ruhr region; the smaller Arbed Saarstahl from the Saarland; and the diversified engineering corporation Mannesmann. The industry was highly efficient and had developed new product lines. It found itself, however, in difficulty from the mid-1970s as a result of increasing overproduction in the glutted European and world steel market, caused both by the expansion of steel production in the NICs of Asia and South America (in which countries production doubled between 1973-83), and by declining demand for steel within the developed world as new substitute materials were developed. The smaller companies of Arbed-Saarstahl, Kloeckner, Hoesch and Peine-Salzgitter fared most badly during this period: the larger and more efficient Thyssen and Krupp upgraded, moving into special steels, and modernised production processes. They thus remained immune from the steel crisis until between 1981 and 1983.

As problems mounted for Europe's steel industry the EEC intervened in 1977 under Viscount Etienne Davignon, the commissioner for industry. A cartel of steel companies (Eurofer) was established to co-ordinate production and pricing, and surplus capacity was slowly reduced through plant closures in Germany, France and Britain. This gentlemen's agreement based upon voluntary discipline broke down, however, in 1980, when the German firms of Kloeckner and Thyssen began to slash their prices and step up production in a desperate attempt to maintain profitability during a period of sharply declining demand. The German firms' actions backfired, however, when Viscount Davignon, facing pressure from Italy, Britain and France, took increased powers into his hands in October 1980 and tightened the Commission's control over the European steel industry. Production quotas were now set for each company, price levels were fixed (at higher levels) and cuts in capacity were determined from Brussels, with the sanction of heavy fines for firms which breached these limits. These measures resulted in a reduction in German steel firms' output and capacity by almost 40% between 1974−82.

Further reductions were carried out between 1983−5 as the recession deepened. These combined measures meant that between 1974 and 1985 total West German steel output fell from 50 million tonnes per annum to only 35 million tonnes. Efforts were made by the government throughout this period to encourage modernisation and rationalisation through the merger of individual companies and government grants, amounting to DM 3 billion between 1983 and 1985 (the majority of which went to Arbed Saarstahl), were provided in an effort to smooth this transition. Following such drastic surgery — which involved the loss of more than 20 000 jobs between 1983-5 alone — German steel firms began to turn the corner of profitability in 1984.[1] Production of special steels was stepped up and companies diversified in an

---

[1] Federal subsidies to the West German steel industry ceased in 1986.

attempt to move into more profitable areas. The most spectacular diversification occurred at Mannesmann, which moved completely out of steel during the early 1970s, transferring into engineering and electronics, and at Thyssen, steel accounting for 56% of its sales in 1974 but only 33% in 1985.

Despite such re-organisation and rationalisation, the longer term future for the German steel industry remains disturbing, faced, as it is, by continuing overcapacity in a glutted and subsidised world steel market and by the progressive decline of traditional steel consuming heavy industries. Two such industries have been the shipbuilding industry and the automobile industry.

In the shipbuilding industry West Germany met with competition from Japan as early as the 1950s. While Germany's share of the world market for new shipping decreased from 17% in 1956 to 7% in 1968, Japan's share increased from 24% to 49%: a share which it still held in 1980. Advanced high productivity manufacturing techniques and the growth in the merchant fleet of South-East Asia were the two factors which explained this movement. The West German shipbuilding industry — centred in the old northern Hanseatic cities of Bremen, Hamburg and Kiel and employing 71 000 in 1975 — faced with a declining market share, was forced to re-direct production towards new lines, such as container ships, roll-on ferries, gas transporters, oil rigs and power station boilers. Much of this diversification was successful. This did not, however, prevent the industry from being seriously damaged by the 1973−4 and 1979−80 oil price hikes and the ensuing economic recession which reduced the volume of world trade at a time when new shipping and container capacity was being developed in the NICs. The world shipbuilding order book slumped between 1974 and 1978 from 129 million gross registered tons (grt) to a miserly 28 million grt, and the portion captured by West Germany fell from 7.35 million to barely 0.5 million grt. Major yard closures became necessary, with in Hamburg the workforce being more than halved from 35 000 to 15 000. This naturally had a deleterious 'knock-on' effect on the troubled steel industry of the Ruhr and Lower Saxony.

The expansion of the West German car industry — based around the huge Volkswagen-Audi corporation (the fifth major car producer in the world, producing 1.88 million vehicles in 1984), Ford, Opel (a General Motors' subsidiary), Daimler-Benz (also Europe's major, and most profitable, lorry producer), BMW and Porsche — created thousands of new jobs during the boom years of the 1950s and 1960s. By 1974 the industry was the third largest in the world (producing 3.6 million vehicles and standing behind the US and Japan). It employed almost 600 000 workers and was the second largest export sector (behind mechanical engineering) in the West German economy, with its output enjoying an enviable reputation for quality, fuel efficiency, engine power and reliability. By comparative European standards the German motor industry was strong and profitable as it entered the 1974−84 recession. During the recession, however, demand for new vehicles stagnated in West Germany at a level of 2.1−2.2 million cars per annum. At the same time, German car producers faced sharpening competition from Japanese producers both at home — the Japanese share rising from only 2% in 1977 to 12% in 1980 in what remains an unusually open market — and abroad in the lucrative American and overseas market, to which almost 60% of West German motor industry production was orientated. The Japanese firms offered attractive, streamlined low-cost models, with the inducements of substantial discounts and special extras.

The European and American car markets were glutted by the early 1980s, with an overcapacity of almost 25%. Prices and profit margins were slashed in response, as the motor industry entered a cannibalistic crisis period between 1980−4, from which German car firms were not immune. The most seriously affected West German concerns were the American subsidiaries Ford and Opel, whose operations were limited to Western Europe. They recorded substantial losses between 1980−3 and were forced to close down plants, with the consequent destruction of 16 000 jobs. The German firms of Volkswagen, Daimler-Benz and BMW proved less willing to shed labour. Volkswagen, the mass lower and middle market producer, which recorded its first losses during the energy crisis of 1974−5, fell even further into the red in 1982 and 1983. In response, Volkswagen stepped up its export efforts in overseas and underdeveloped markets — entering into agreements to open new plants in East Germany, Spain and China, to add to its extensive activities in the United States and Brazil — and it began to learn from Japanese production techniques and marketing ploys, adding new extra features to these export models. Its fuel-efficient Golf model proved to be particularly successful. BMW and Daimler-Benz, with a secure hold over the high quality upper-range market, were less seriously affected by the recession, but they sought greater security by diversifying into middle-range and fuel-efficient diesel models and into other industries.

West Germany's car firms began to emerge out of the worst of the recession by 1984 and, with a boom in exports to the United States — helped by the weak Deutsche Mark — they began recording improving profit returns, with balance sheets now in the black. Their fortunes further improved in 1985 and 1986 as home demand picked up. German firms, with the exception of Ford Werke, proved themselves able to cope with NIC competition, the switch to lead-free petrol and the catalytic convertor, and the rise in labour costs which followed the damaging 1984 IG Metall strike. Thus by 1985 West German car production had increased to over 3.8 million vehicles and, although substantial investment had been made in automation, the labour force began to expand once more, reaching a level of 700 000.

West Germany's major industry, mechanical engineering and machine tools, which employs more than one million workers and produces 18% of the country's exports, passed more comfortably through the 1974−84 recession. It faced increasing competition from the Japanese in the lower range of mass produced machine tools, but retained its lead in higher quality, custom built machinery. During the years between 1974 and 1980 a boom in exports to the Middle East oil countries helped maintain the profitability of Germany's leading engineering firms — GHH, Krupp, Thyssen, Deutsche Babcock and Mannesmann — enabling them to dip into their accumulated reserves to ride out the sharp 1980−3 recession. Upgrading and diversification away from seamless steam tubes and into electronics, aerospace, information systems and environmental protection equipment enabled Mannesmann to record net profits throughout this troubled decade. West Germany's chemical and electronics industries suffered more severely.

The electronics industry met with particularly fierce competition from Japan and the NICs in audio and visual lines and from Dutch and Italian firms in consumer durable lines. In 1970 foreign penetration of the German market had reached only 14%, by 1980 it had risen to 32%. In certain lines, such as the manufacture of black and white televisions, West German firms were forced to concede defeat and cease competing with lower cost overseas suppliers. Siemens (Europe's second largest electronics company) and Grundig managed to maintain profitability, though at a reduced level and with reductions in manpower levels, and engaged in tie-up deals with the Dutch giant Philips in the expanding video recorder, office automation and micro-chip sector. AEG-Telefunken, however, after recording successive losses from 1973

101

onwards, was forced into the hands of the official receiver (*Vergleich*) in September 1982. The prime factor behind this decline was the loss made in the competitive consumer electronics sector. This was compounded by AEG's unfortunate involvement in the Siberian pipeline and a number of nuclear power station projects. After 1983 AEG hobbled along as a slimmed-down concern, supported by government credits and asset sales. Its television and hi-fi manufacturing wing Telefunken was sold to the French Thomson group and 49% of AEG's stake in its word-processing subsidiary, Olympia Werke, was temporarily sold to a banking consortium. By 1985, however, shorn of its loss making consumer durables division, AEG had recovered. It had paid off a substantial portion of its debts, recaptured its stake in Olympia and was recording healthy profits as a leaner and more specialised concern.

In the chemical industry West Germany, with three (BASF, Bayer and Hoechst) of the world's top four companies, was the world's second largest chemical producer, holding an 18% share of the global market. This industry was, however, undermined by the oil price hikes of the 1970s — which sharply increased raw material input costs — and by the severe contraction in demand for chemicals during the 1980–4 recession. The profits of Germany's chemical firms were more than halved between 1980–2, as factories were forced to work at two-thirds capacity and to sell products at artifically low prices. The largest losses were in the petrochemicals, bulk chemicals and plastics divisions, where competition was growing from new producers in the oil rich countries of the Middle East. This particularly affected BASF. Bayer and Hoechst, involved to a greater degree in pharmaceuticals, paints, agricultural chemicals and speciality plastics, were better able to ride out the recession. The closure of a number of unprofitable ventures (such as polyethylene and pvc) and an upgrading into specialist markets restored the profitability of Germany's chemical giants in 1984 to pre-1980 levels. However, future prospects in the traditional 'heavy chemical' divisions remain bleak for West Germany's oil deficient companies, which will need to continue to upgrade and diversify.

West Germany's traditional industries, while fitter and stronger than many of their European rivals, were clearly severely affected by the 1974–84 economic recession and by the heightened competition from low cost producers in Japan and the NICs. Firms were forced to re-think their production methods and market strategy and to slim down their workforce and modernise their plant. This sometimes involved moving the production of component items to lesser developed, low wage countries, adding further to the loss of jobs in German factories. The broad balance and base of the West German economy, with its nucleus of engineering, steel, electrical and chemical industries, remained in place in 1986, but it had contracted in size and had been forced to change and upgrade product mixes. Government involvement in the economy had also increased with the granting of subsidies — although still low by comparative standards — to ailing concerns in the shipbuilding, steel and electrical industries. Overall, manufacturing's share of the workforce had declined, while that of services had increased.

A more dramatic re-structuring of the German economy, with the growth of new 'high-tech' industries, was also becoming apparent by 1986. West Germany's electrical, engineering, automobile, steel and chemical giants began to expand into the new spheres of aerospace, micro-technology, automation and bio-technology as a rash of mergers took place in 1985 and 1986: the most prominent of which was Daimler-Benz's take-over of AEG. The smaller firms of Olympia and Nixdorf were also making a major impact in the office machines and computer markets. West Germany still remained far behind Japan and California in these new high-tech and high growth sectors and would need to remodel its organisational approach if the gap was to be fully bridged. It needed to foster an industrial culture geared towards invention as well as innovation and to encourage small scale entrepreneurs and 'intrapreneurs'. Greater state research investment and pan-industrial and pan-national co-operation was also required in a number of costly, pathbreaking fields: the technical tie-up between Siemens and Philips in micro-chip research being a promising example of this. Such developments have thus far, however, largely been concentrated in the southern states and have served to accentuate regional divisions as German industry has begun a progressive movement away from its traditional centres in the north.

## Regional Changes — the Movement South

Regional differences in income levels have remained low in West Germany when compared, for example, with the North-South divides evident in contemporary Italy or the United Kingdom. Traditionally the richest regions in the republic were the industrial

Länder of North-Rhine-Westphalia and Hesse, in which states was situated the Rhine-Ruhr colliery and steel mill belt. It was here, and in portions of the more northerly Länder, where Germany's primary industries were located, being positioned at the centre of the vast European market, well served by waterway and land transportation networks — the East-West *Hellweg* and the northward-flowing Rhine river. With the decline, however, of traditional industries during the 1974−84 recession, the northern Länder became depressed, recording unemployment rates in excess of 10% in 1984. By contrast, during the same period, the attractive southern Länder of Baden-Württemberg and Bavaria became new centres of industrial growth, drawing in migrants from the north and exhibiting unemployment rates of under 6%. The German economy was moving southwards.

During the 1950s, Baden-Württemberg and Bavaria remained poor and relatively backward, small-farmer, agricultural states containing only a few industrial nuclei in Karlsruhe, Stuttgart and Munich. These two states, however, topped the Länder growth league from the mid-1960s, catching up, before recently passing, the northern Länder in terms of income per capita. In Bavaria, utilising cheap labour drawn from local agriculture and Gastarbeiter brought in from Yugoslavia, modern electrical goods, electronics, aerospace and arms industries were set up, as well as the up-market motor manufacturing firm of BMW. In Baden-Württemberg, which inherited a decaying textile industry, the quality car and truck giant Mercedes-Benz and the sports car manufacturer Porsche were established, in addition to investment goods industries manned by industrious local Swabians. These two souther Länder did not inherit the weight of older and declining traditional industries which dragged down the northern states. The heavier industries which they did possess, for example the car manufacturers BMW and Mercedes-Benz and the engineers GHH, continued to expand and take on additional labour during the 1970s recession. It has, however, been flexible smaller and medium sized firms (*Mittelstände*) and modern 'high-tech' concerns which have been the dynamic engine of growth in Baden-Württemberg and Bavaria since the mid-1970s. The cluster of universities, industrial and defence research establishments around Munich and Stuttgart helped create a small *'Silzium Tal'* bustling with workshops producing data-processing, micro-electronics and computer equipment. Munich, the home of Siemens, the aircraft firm Messerschmitt-Bolkow-Blohm, the silicon producer Wacker

Chimie and the US companies Texas Instruments and Digital Equipment, has been an important 'growth pole'. The CDU and CSU state leaders, Lothar Späth and Franz-Josef Strauss, favouring a mixture of deregulationary free-enterprise and interventionist state tax concession and infra-structural support, in terms of research facilities and communications, have aided this growth process.[1] The completion of the Rhine-Main-Danube canal, opening up full waterborne communication between Rotterdam and the Black Sea through Regensburg in Bavaria, will add further impetus to industrial growth in southern Germany.

By contrast the older industrial north has been forced to painfully restructure itself during these years of recession. In these Länder were located the declining shipbuilding industry, the problem car firms Ford and Opel, and the troubled steel mills which had played a vital role in West German economic growth during the 'miracle years'. The cities of Bremen, Hamburg and isolated Berlin (dependent on central government for handouts of DM 3.6 million per annum — equivalent to half its budget total) and the Saarland were particularly seriously affected. (See Table 14.)

**Table 14 The North-South Divide in Contemporary West Germany**

| Land | (1986) Unemployment Rate % | (1984) (DM'000) GNP per Capita | (1980) (DM million) Receipts (+) From or Payments (−) Länder Compensation Fund |
|---|---|---|---|
| North | | | |
| Schleswig-Holstein | 10.3 | 25.8 | + 320 |
| Hamburg | 12.9 | 44.1 | − 304 |
| Bremen | 15.7 | 30.6 | + 179 |
| Lower Saxony | 11.1 | 25.2 | + 748 |
| North-Rhine-Westphalia | 10.8 | 28.4 | − 79 |
| Centre | | | |
| Saarland | 13.2 | 24.3 | + 284 |
| Hesse | 6.6 | 29.9 | − 299 |
| Rhineland-Palatinate | 7.9 | 26.2 | + 246 |
| South | | | |
| Bavaria | 5.9 | 27.8 | + 401 |
| Baden-Württemberg | 4.9 | 30.9 | −1496 |
| National Average | 8.6 | 28.7 | — |

[1]In Bavaria Franz-Josef Strauss helped build up the aerospace industry, his state government promoting the European Airbus project and taking a 7% shareholding in MBB.

Within the old Rhine-Ruhr industrial belt there were sub-regional shifts with production moving away from the Ruhr interior (Essen and Dortmund) towards the Rhineland cities which were served by cheap water communications. This formed part of a longer term process of decline for east-central Germany, which was cut off after 1945 by partition from traditional markets and supply sources to the east. Within the Rhineland, Düsseldorf emerged as a nuclei for modern and often Japanese-owned new industries, being the site for 300 of the 450 Japanese firms established in West Germany and housing a local Japanese community amounting to more than 6000. In Hamburg and Bremen, production diversified away from maritime industries with, for example, the establishment of an MBB aerospace works and a huge 250 000 cars-a-year Daimler-Benz factory (employing 10 000) in Bremen in 1984, and in West Berlin a high-tech renaissance was in evidence by 1986. Inside the decaying inner cities, however, considerable social problems and tensions emerged, including racial conflicts directed against the large Gastarbeiter communities and squatter conflicts over housing shortages.

The movement south in the West German economy created new problems of fairly apportioning regional development aid as re-distribution formulas were too slowly adjusted to the new conditions and as conservative alliances in the Bundesrat blocked changes in the regulations. The Ruhr, in particular, remained unfairly treated until the Constitutional Court ruled in June 1986 that changes should be effected in the *Finanzausgleich* tax system. Depression in the north and growth in the south produced, in addition, diverging trends in national politics. This was highlighted by the 1985 Länder elections in the Saarland and North-Rhine Westphalia, which resulted in resounding victories for the SPD advocating firm interventionist policies to support ailing industries and to improve the infra-structure of these northern states. Such policies contrasted with the de-regulationary policies favoured by the popular Späth and Strauss in the CDU-CSU controlled south.

## Policy Differences and the Breakdown of Economic Consensus

The divergent policy prescriptions offered by the SPD and by the CDU-CSU-FDP coalition in the March 1983 election campaign illustrated the breakdown in the consensus which had embraced approaches to the West German economy since the mid-1960s. The SPD and CDU had never offered identical programmes during the years between 1966 and 1982, but differences had been only slight. Both parties favoured, after the 'total state' experience of the Nazi era, leaving the economy to the operation of free-market forces and to competitive private companies, while the government pursued a tight fiscal policy to provide a stable environment with low inflation and a secure currency. Thus by comparative European standards the German economy was notable for its 'open' nature, for the limited extent of state participation in and support given to the industrial sector, and for its semi-privatised welfare system. The SPD and CDU differed by degrees in their enthusiasm for fiscal dabbling, selective intervention and welfare support — the SPD favouring greater intervention to iron out inequalities and injustices: the CDU prefering to leave matters to the marketplace — with the FDP playing a significant role in bridging the differences and pushing the SPD, when in power, closer than they would have chosen towards a traditional liberal economic stance.

The budgets of the years between 1974 and 1985 showed a constant concern to maintain fiscal rectitude and low budgetary deficits. Only in 1975 and 1978 was a reflationary demand boost sanctioned. Chancellor Schmidt, in close personal contact with leading industrialists and financiers and with the controller of the Bundesbank, played a prominent role in this economic strategy. Hans Apel, Hans Matthöfer and Manfred Lahnstein from the SPD headed the Finance Ministry and Hans Friderichs and Otto Lambsdorff from the FDP controlled the important Economics Ministry, ensuring that coalition policy did not sway too far from a 'hands-off', free-market course.

After 1982, however, significant differences emerged between the two parties over approaches to the economy. The SPD now came to favour introducing a sizable job creation package to deal with the economic crisis, financed, if necessary, through tax increases and through a larger budget deficit. In addition, the SPD, drawing its support from West Germany's ailing industrial regions, accepted the need to extend temporary aid to the country's troubled, traditional industries to give them the opportunity to modernise and re-organise their production processes. The CDU, CSU and FDP, by contrast, remained committed to controlling and reducing the budget deficit through tight fiscal and monetary control and they remained hostile to the idea of state subsidies for troubled industries. More radical elements within these parties, including the Economics Ministers, Lambsdorff and Bangemann, and Finance Minister Stoltenberg, favoured de-regulating and freeing the economy even further — through taxation reform, privatisation, the setting of targets for the reduction of government spending, and the abolition of restrictive controls on enterprise.

The implementation of this new 'neo-liberal' strategy proved at first to be slow and halting. Between 1983 and 1985 significant cuts in welfare spending were made and rent controls were eased, but only part of one company, VEBA AG, had been sold to the private sector, while political pressures forced the grant of substantial subsidies to the ailing coal, steel and shipbuilding industries.[1] It gained momentum, however, in 1986 with the unveiling of a major schedule of privatisation — involving the sale of the remaining federal government stake in VEBA and Volkswagen and part of its stake in VIAG, Prakla-Seismos and IVG — the introduction of tax cuts, the reduction in industrial subsidies and the reform of the labour law. This Reaganite-Thatcherite programme will be further extended following the CDU-CSU-FDP coalition's re-election in 1987, endangering the consensual basis of the West German postwar 'social market economy'.

A second and more serious fissure emerged after 1978 in the co-operative 'Concerted Action' consensus which had been built up between West Germany's government (federal and Land), trade unions and industrial and financial groups. 'Concerted Action' set out the need for all major groupings which exercised economic responsibility to work together in the formulation and execution of economic policy — meeting annually to set guidelines for wages, prices and economic growth. This depended upon the supply of reliable information to the participants, from which they could make informed and sensible judgements; upon a consensus existing for the policies being pursued; and upon each side, particularly the trade unions, being able to deliver their promises. The first pre-requisite, trustworthy economic information, was supplied regularly by West Germany's five economic research institutes and by the Council of Economic Advisers; the second, political consensus, by the lack of class differentiation in postwar Germany. The last requirement, the ability of trade unions to adhere to broad agreements, derived from the structure of the labour movement in West Germany. There existed one major supra-union body, the

---

[1]Privatisation plans for Lufthansa airlines also had to be shelved as a result of the strong opposition of Franz-Josef Strauss.

DGB (*Deutscher Gewerkschaftsbund*) (the German equivalent of the TUC, though more powerful), which incorporated 7.8 million members connected with 17 member unions, including IG-Metall with its 2.6 million members involved in a broad range of industries.[1] West German trade union concentration contrasted with the diffuse British craft unions. It was thus possible in West Germany for union leaders to enforce discipline and ensure that bargains were honoured. This was most evident between 1966 and 1978, with union bosses delivering productivity increases and industrial peace, their members gaining in return a share of the economic prosperity built up during these growth years and an increasing voice in company affairs with the spread of 'industrial co-determination' (*Mitbestimmung* — workers' participation).

This consensus began to break down, however, with the onset of recession and the end of the era of full employment. The unions, after a brief surge in wages during the mid-1970s, were called increasingly to bear the brunt of austerity measures and to accept declining shares of the national cake during the years between 1976−9. Employers, meanwhile, seeking to push ahead with the introduction of new labour-saving technology and shed excess manpower, objected to union attempts to block this process through the influence they exerted under the 'co-determination' system.

'Co-determination' was a form of industrial partnership which provided for almost equal representation of shareholders and workers on companies' supervisory boards — the balance was tilted narrowly in the employer's favour since the chairman with a casting vote was nominated by the shareholders and one employee representative had to be drawn from senior management. It was applied to the coal and steel industry in 1951 (where full parity existed with a neutral chairman) and was extended to all firms with workforces in excess of 2000 between 1976−8.[2] Some companies attempted to get round the regulations by changing their corporate status or breaking down their operations into smaller units. However, the German employers' federation (BDA — *Bundesvereinigung der Deutschen Arbeitgeberverände*) decided to challenge this new law in the Federal Constitutional Court on the grounds that it violated the constitutional guarantee of the

[1]30% of West German workers belong to trade unions compared to 42% in Britain and 15% in the United States and France.

[2]In companies with less than 2 000 employees the unions are entitled to only a third of the seats on the supervisory board.

right to own and freely use property. The Constitutional Court subsequently ruled (in March 1979) that the new law was legitimate, but that co-determination should go no further. The employers' action had served in the meantime, however, to worsen an already deteriorating industrial relations climate and persuaded the unions to withdraw from the tripartite 'concerted action' committee in July 1977 — attending only informally in subsequent years.

A spate of strikes during 1978 — involving the engineering and steelworkers' union, IG Metall, and the militant printing workers' union, IG Druck und Papier — further soured relations. The management responded by resorting to 'lock-outs', increasing the numbers of workers affected to thus stretch union resources. These tactics proved largely successful and almost bankrupted IG Druck, who after calling out 2000 workers in five newspaper plants had finally to support 32 000 workers in 500 firms throughout the country as a result of management lockouts. IG Metall and IG Druck challenged the use of this strike-breaking weapon, taking their case to the Federal Labour Court in Kassel. The court ruled, however, in June 1980 that 'lock-outs' were legitimate, although they should bear a 'reasonable relationship' to the extent of the strike, involving a similar number to those on official strike.

The 1978 engineering strike, like earlier disputes in 1976, revolved around the traditional issue of pay. In contrast, the printing and steel strikes of 1978 centred upon the introduction of new technology and its threat to job security. This was to become a key issue for the West German labour movement during the following six years, with IG Metall at the forefront of this new struggle.

IG Metall, concerned at the rapid contraction of the workforce in the steel industry as firms rationalised and modernised, began to press for the introduction of a 35-hour working week and the inclusion of an extra time shift as a means of stabilising employment. This was rejected by the steel employers in 1978 who argued that it would cost the troubled industry the equivalent of a 20% pay rise and disastrously reduce its international competitiveness. The most they would offer was six weeks annual paid holiday. This was rejected by IG Metall who called out 37 000 workers in selected motor industry supply plants in North-Rhine-Westphalia. The steel management responded with 'lock-outs' and a bitter six week dispute — the first in the steel industry since the war — was entered into between November 1978 and January 1979, involving almost 100 000 workers in the Rhine-Ruhr belt. IG Metall held out for their

35-hour week demand until the very last moment, but were finally forced to capitulate, achieving few concessions from management — only a modest pay increase and an extension of paid leave and holidays. This bitterly disappointed the union rank and file, who only narrowly approved the settlement when it went to an end of strike ballot.

The position of West Germany's employers hardened following their victory in the steel dispute. They pressured IG Metall into signing an agreement which fixed their standard week at 40 hours until the end of 1983 (with six weeks paid holidays in return) and the Federation of German Employers (BDA) drew up a 'taboo catalogue' binding all employers not to concede working weeks below this limit. The unions responded in turn by vowing to adopt a firmer stance in future disputes. They failed, however, to carry this threat through. In the 1979 and 1980 pay rounds IG Metall and the public services union (OTV), after engaging in token stoppages, backed down from major industrial action and accepted wage increases close to the inflation mark.[1] This set an upper standard and forced smaller unions to accept cuts in real wages throughout the period between 1979 and 1983.

The West German union movement thus faced, as in other West European countries, a difficult five years after 1979 as its membership and political influence diminished during a recession period.[2] From the winter of 1983, however, with the IG Metall 40-hour week agreement due for expiry and with engineering firms returning to profitability, the ground was prepared for a resumption of the fight for a shortened 35-hour week. This struggle promised to be prolonged and bitter as a result of the accession to power of the sterner CDU-CSU-FDP government and the movement up the union ranks of a younger and more radical generation of leaders, for example Franz Steinkühler, IG Metall's deputy leader. The Federal Chancellor, Helmut Kohl, and his popular Labour Minister, Norbert Blüm (a former Opel factory worker who was on the moderate 'labour wing' of the CDU), at first attempted in December 1983 to head off a dispute by introducing, as compensation, a state-assisted scheme for early retirement at the age of 59 (instead of at between 63 and 65). However IG Metall rejected this proposal and, with the support of the DGB and the post, printing, banking and railway

[1]IG Metall and the OTV put in claims of 9-10% in 1979, but settled for 6.5% coupled with a lengthening of holiday allowances. In 1980 IG Metall initially demanded an 8% pay rise, but were forced to accept one of only 3.2%.
[2]Membership of the DGB fell from 7.9 million in 1981 to 7.6 million in 1985.

unions, continued to press for its 35-hour week. It gained the support of the SPD, whose chairman Willy Brandt firmly backed the principle of the shortened week at a major rally in February 1984. The CDU, by contrast, backed the employers. This brought to an end the postwar tradition of party neutralism during industrial disputes and turned the 35-hour week into a highly charged ideological issue.

The IG Metall union engaged in 69 regional and two national negotiating meetings during March and April 1985 in an attempt to reach a compromise solution. They were willing to seek ways of phasing in a movement towards the 35-hour week. But the *Gesamtmetall* employers' federation, backed by the CDU government, took an uncompromising stand, sticking firmly to the principle of a 40-hour week to maintain West German industry's competitiveness. IG Metall were thus forced, after winning the necessary 75% majority in ballots, to take strike action in May 1984. They had prepared in advance for the strike, having built up a strike fund of DM 500 million, and they concentrated on a number of target strikes against prosperous employers in specific regions — against Daimler-Benz and Porsche in Baden-Württemberg; against Siemens in Frankfurt; and against Opel, engineering firms and car component manufacturers in Hesse — instead of calling a crippling, national strike. Further support was provided by the print union IG Druck, which engaged in sporadic strike activity between April and July.

The engineering-metalworking strike, however, became lengthier, costlier and more extensive than IG Metall had envisaged as a result of the firm stance adopted by management and the government. Employers retaliated to the union's selective strikes with 'lock outs' and lay offs once again. In the past, under the previous SPD administration, such laid off workers had been awarded unemployment pay by the Federal Labour Institute — a tripartite body, comprising management, unions and government, in which the government held the deciding vote. In 1984, however, the CDU-CSU-FDP government sided with management and vetoed the payment of short-term unemployment benefits to workers made idle by the effects of strikes elsewhere. This decision burdened IG Metall with unexpected additional liabilities and stretched the union's funds, which were already being rapidly reduced by the burden of official strike pay (set at a level 70% of normal pay). The strike dragged on for seven weeks and eventually involved 1.5 million workers and thus ranked as West Germany's most serious postwar industrial dispute — resulting in the loss of DM 10 billion in production (equivalent to 0.5% of GDP), including 380 000 motor vehicles. The dispute ended at the close of June 1984 with a compromise solution — management agreeing to introduce, without loss of pay, a 38.5 hour working week (38 hours in the steel industry) from April 1985.

This represented a partial victory for IG Metall and an important step towards the 35-hour week at the cost though of an embittering of worker-management relations.[1] Employers managed to get round the new 38.5 hour working week regulations by introducing more flexible working patterns and increased overtime, minimising the overall employment impact of the reform. In addition, however, they persuaded the federal government to push through in March 1986 a reform of the National Labour Code to prevent the payment of unemployment benefit to workers indirectly laid off during disputes who later benefited from strike settlements. This measure, aimed at preventing 'striking on the cheap', enraged the unions, who had briefly resumed tripartite 'concerted action' negotiations in September 1985. The DGB pronounced the Labour Minister, Norbert Blüm, to be a 'class traitor' and took the unprecedented step of refusing to allow Chancellor Kohl to address its quadrennial congress in 1986. Protest strikes against the government's new policies were carried out in October and December 1985 and February—March 1986 by the union movement which accused the federal government of seeking a 'permanent conflict' with the forces of labour.

---

[1]This action, coupled with the promotion of the more militant Franz Steinkühler to full leadership of IG Metall, promised to place in jeopardy West Germany's postwar tradition of peaceful social and industrial co-existence.

# Part Four

## FOREIGN POLICY UNDER SCHMIDT AND KOHL

### West German foreign policy interests

Two key issues have dominated West German foreign policy in the postwar decades — the 'German question' and the functioning of the international economy.

### The German Question

With the defeat of Hitler and the sequestration of almost one half of the country by Poland and the GDR after 1945 all hopes of the creation of a *Grossdeutschland* uniting the scattered Germanic tribes of Central Europe appeared to have finally been lost. The Soviet Union, United States and West Germany's Western European neighbours sought to maintain the two Germanies as weakened and divided nations in the interests of future peace in Europe. Within West Germany, however, the goal of re-unification was sustained by the existence of a substantial refugee and 'expellee' community and by the demands of the Basic Law. The 'German question' became the pre-eminent issue in German foreign affairs, with re-unification in 'peace and freedom' the foremost goal.

During the 1950s and early 1960s opinions differed as to the best route to take in pursuance of this goal. Konrad Adenauer, seeking to first rehabilitate the country and gain acceptance by the Western alliance and concerned with the danger of the spread of communism, supported the United States in its hard-line policy against the Soviet Union — seeking to eventually negotiate German re-unification from a position of strength. This policy involved joining NATO (1955), accepting re-armament and refusing to formally recognise the illegitimate puppet regimes of Eastern Europe (the Hallstein Doctrine). The SPD, however, criticised this stance as being essentially flawed — driving the two halves of Germany further and further apart. The erection of the Berlin Wall in August 1961 and America's subsequent meek acceptance gave support to this interpretation and prompted a re-assessment of German foreign policy during the early 1960s.

The views of both the SPD and the CDU began now to converge as a new 'policy of movement' (*Bewegungspolitik*) was devised during the mid 1960s, involving a thawing in relations (diplomatic and trading) with the Eastern bloc nations — excluding East Germany. This policy, however, ran into opposition from the Soviet Union, which viewed it, in the wake of the 1968 Czech crisis, as being essentially divisive, destabilising Eastern Europe. A more radical re-appraisal of the 'German Question' was thus called for and was carried out by the SPD and FDP.

They recognised that, after more than twenty years, major changes had occurred within Eastern Europe and that the possibility of rapid and peaceful German re-unification was now remote. In such circumstances, it was argued that a realistic attempt should be made to harmonise and normalise relations with West Germany's eastern neighbours and to improve conditions for Germans living in the GDR — opening up the borders for the movement of families and friends. In the short run, it was felt that this increased contact and co-operation would prevent a further drifting apart of the two Germanies. In the long run, it was hoped that such 'change through rapprochement' would bring a convergence between the economic and social systems of the two countries, so that political barriers would eventually wither away. Willy Brandt, Egon Bahr and the FDP leader, Walter Scheel, were the key figures behind the formulation of this new conciliatory Ostpolitik. It fitted in with the more general climate of detente which was extending between the USSR under Leonid Brezhnev and the United States under Richard Nixon, and with the decline in popular concern for German re-unification as a new and distinctive West German 'free-market' nationality developed in contradistinction to the communist evolution of the GDR.

The establishment of full diplomatic relations with Romania in 1967, in contravention of the Hallstein Doctrine, marked the first step in this new Ostpolitik. Even more significant departures were made following the coming to power of the new SPD-FDP coalition. Thus, in 1970, treaties were entered into normalising relations with the Soviet Union and Poland (recognising the Oder-Neisse line); in 1971 the Four Power Berlin Agreement secured access to West Berlin; and in September 1972 a 'Basic Treaty' was signed with East Germany — recognising the GDR's frontiers and separate existence. This came close to giving full recognition, but stopped short of acknowledging a separate East German nationality (permanent missions were stationed in Bonn and East Berlin instead of ambassadors). The CDU remained critical that too much had been conceded and too little gained, but it did not block the new treaties in the Bundesrat. It was left to the CSU, led by Franz-Josef

Strauss, to fight the legality of the treaties in the Federal Constitutional Court in 1973, but without success. Ostpolitik — opening up human and commercial frontiers between the East and West — had become the new consensus in West German foreign policy.

## Economic factors in West German foreign policy

The West German economy is outward looking, depending heavily upon foreign trade. It imports raw mineral and energy inputs and foodstuffs, and exports manufactures to the value of almost 30% of its GNP. (See p. 97 for a regional breakdown of these exports.) Successive administrations have thus been anxious to maintain friendly and peaceful international relations and to push for liberalisation in tariff policies. West Germany's entry into the European Coal and Steel Community (1952) and the European Economic Community (1957) were clear and successful indications of this desire. Although remaining a net contributor to the EEC budget — to the value of 1.8 billion ecu in 1981 — West Germany gained tremendous commercial and political advantages from its membership — the EEC providing both the largest single market for its manufactured goods and a platform for the German voice in international affairs. Eastern Europe and the Middle East became other areas of economic and political importance for West Germany from the 1960s.

As it became rehabilitated into the international community — signalled by its acceptance into the United Nations in 1973 — and as its economic power continued to expand during the 1960s, so West Germany began to play a more important role on the world stage. Lacking the colonial responsibilities of Britain or France, its direct global interests remained limited. But at world economic summits (instituted in 1975 by Giscard d'Estaing) West Germany's voice, as the third largest economy in the West and enjoying large trading surpluses to the value of more than $10 billion per annum (1967–78), was listened to with respect and its influence upon policy prescriptions progressively increased.

# West German Foreign Policy: 1976–1987

## Ostpolitik after the fall of Brandt

Some of the initial optimism and enthusiasm surrounding the new Ostpolitik had waned by the mid-1970s, with the realisation that there were clear limits to Eastern concessions. Links between West Berlin and West Germany were improved, but the Berlin Wall remained and severe restrictions were still placed upon movement from the GDR to the Federal Republic, as East Germany, while grateful for finally obtaining international recognition and while seeking to raise living standards through expanded trade, sought also to protect its embryonic social and political system from undermining by the West.[1] Thus, under Helmut Schmidt and the FDP foreign minister, Hans-Dietrich Genscher, Ostpolitik detente was carried out with greater caution and scepticism. Progress continued, however, to be made — new supplementary treaties were signed with East Germany and Poland in 1975 and 1976: the treaty with Poland providing for the re-settlement of 120 000 German nationals living in Poland wishing to move to the Federal Republic in return for a 'transfer fee'.

It was, however, in the economic sphere where progress and co-operation went furthest. Aided by substantial West German concessions (for example, the 'swing' overdraft facility, the 1978 Traffic Agreement and the 1979 Long Term Trading Agreement) inter-German trade increased substantially — expanding at an annual rate of 14% between 1969 and 1976. Increased market and investment outlets were created for West German manufacturers, particularly during the mid 1970s, with Comecon's share of West Germany's exports rising from 5½% in 1970 to 9% in 1975. Aided by its geographical position, West Germany became the major single external trading partner for Eastern Europe. However, the major beneficiaries of this 'economic detente' were the East Germans, who granted a number of limited humanitarian concessions in return for large financial subsidies and a substantial improvement in their domestic living standards.

The pursuit of conciliatory Ostpolitik and economic detente during the early and mid 1970s did not, however, signal any weakening in West Germany's commitment to the United States and the NATO alliance. It firmly supported the United States in its plans for a neutron bomb (later shelved by President Carter in 1978)

[1] The FRG-GDR Traffic Treaty of 1972 allowed for the free movement of West German citizens to East Germany to visit relatives and for tourism, subject to compulsory daily currency exchange limits. It only, however, allowed East German pensioners (men over the age of 65, women over the age of 60) to visit West Germany and West Berlin. Thus during the 1970s around 8 million West Germans visited East Germany each year, while only 1.3 million East Germans moved in the opposite direction.

and was a prime instigator behind the NATO nuclear weapons 'modernisation programme' of November 1979 — Chancellor Schmidt viewing the maintenance of a credible balance of deterrence as essential both to guarantee the security of West Germany and West Berlin and to maintain pressure on the Soviet Union to make genuine concessions in the fields of human rights and armament levels.

US-Soviet relations had been comparatively amicable during the 1970s, allowing room for the West Germans to develop their own form of Ostpolitik detente with the Eastern bloc. After 1980, however, American attitudes hardened once more following the Soviet invasion of Afghanistan (December 1979), the troubles in Poland and the accession to the presidency of the Republican, Ronald Reagan (January 1981). This new 'cold war' atmosphere developed during a period of gathering world recession which, with mounting Comecon debts and narrowing export markets, caused a sharp contraction in East-West trade. (The Comecon bloc's share of West Germany's exports declined to only 6% in 1981.) Both factors meant that the maintenance of Ostpolitik detente became increasingly difficult during the years between 1980−5.

In 1980 President Carter and the US administration called for economic sanctions against both Iran (who were holding American citizens hostage at the US embassy in Teheran) and the Soviet Union, following their invasion of Afghanistan. Chancellor Schmidt, who disdained President Carter as a naive and unpredictable amateur in international affairs, and foreign minister Genscher eventually supported the United States in these actions — restricting high-technology sales to the Soviet Union and boycotting the forthcoming Moscow Olympics — but this was only after considerable dithering and delay. The West German government aimed to maintain bridges between East and West and prevent a full return to 'cold war' isolationism and militarism. Thus, while supporting the United States in its sanctions and boycotts and while strengthening NATO's Turkish ally with a substantial aid package, Schmidt and Genscher continued to meet the Soviet leader, Leonid Brezhnev, in July 1980 — entering into a 25-year agreement on economic cooperation — and arranged largescale measures of economic support to prop up the tottering Polish regime of Edward Gierek. Inter-German contacts were also maintained. Although at the height of the Polish crisis in August 1980 the planned meeting between Helmut Schmidt and the East German leader, Erich

Honecker, was cancelled and in October 1980 (five days before the Bundestag elections) the compulsory exchange limit for West German visitors to the GDR was drastically raised from DM 13 to DM 25 a day, deterring entry, top level talks were resumed fourteen months later. Little was achieved, but Ostpolitik, though stagnating, was kept alive, with both sides — the East Germans for economic reasons, the West Germans for political reasons — anxious to maintain the dialogue during a troubled period for superpower relations.

Between 1982 and 1984, US-Soviet relations reached their lowest point since the Cuban missiles crisis of 1961, as the date (December 1983) for the stationing of NATO's new medium range nuclear missiles in Western Europe approached, martial law was declared in Poland (December 1981) and Soviet troops remained stationed in Afghanistan. The uncompromising stance adopted by President Reagan towards Soviet actions imperilled the whole superstructure of detente and Ostpolitik and placed the West German government in a difficult position during these years. While remaining loyal, despite considerable internal party opposition, to the Pershing-II deployment decision, Helmut Schmidt and Hans-Dietrich Genscher began to take a partly independent line and failed to acquiesce in a number of crucial American demands.

The first and most serious German-American rift occurred over reactions to martial law in Poland. The Reagan administration pressed for stern sanctions against both the Soviet Union and the new Polish regime under General Jaruzelski. The Schmidt government, however, while suspending official aid to Poland, accepted the temporary imposition of martial law by the Polish army as a necessary evil to pre-empt direct Russian intervention. It therefore refused to join the US in its wide range of economic sanctions and continued to participate in the huge Siberian pipeline project.[1] The US suspected that pecuniary motives, at a time of economic recession, swayed the German decision. Relations between America and Bonn were further strained by the Schmidt government's failure, as a result of fiscal constraints, to fully keep up with its 1979 NATO pledge to increase its military budget by 3% per annum in 'real terms' during the first half of the 1980s.

These actions coincided with a wave of anti-American demonstrations by the German peace movement and assassinations of

---

[1]France and Britain, who also had engineering firms participating in this project, similarly refused to accede to pressure from the United States, forcing President Reagan to eventually back down.

NATO military personnel by terrorist organisations. Coupled with Soviet talk concerning the 'divisibility of detente', they precipitated American fears that West Germany was being slowly de-coupled from the NATO alliance and becoming neutralised or 'Finlandised'. However, although a number of voices — for example, the Greens and Herbert Wehner of the SPD — inside Germany did dream of a neutral West Germany on good terms with its eastern neighbours, majority opinion in Germany remained firmly committed to the NATO alliance and the United States. They sought only to add a European voice to the East-West dialogue and avoid a blinkered, doctrinaire approach to these issues.

The rift between Washington and Bonn was only temporary. It was healed by the decision of European parliaments, including the Bundestag, to accept the deployment of Cruise and Pershing-II missiles during the winter of 1983, and by the accession of a new CDU-CSU-FDP administration which was more Atlanticist in its outlook, with its defence minister, Manfred Wörner, playing an active role in NATO's modernisation planning. Relations with both the East and West did not fully, however, return to their mid-1970s condition.

The Kohl administration, with Genscher remaining as foreign minister, sought to maintain Ostpolitik (Helmut Kohl visiting the Soviet leader, Yuri Andropov, in Moscow in June 1983) and a neighbourly relationship with East Germany to prove to the electorate that the SPD did not have a monopoly over solutions to the 'German question'. There was a short term deterioration in relations with the Eastern bloc during 1983 — culminating in the retaliatory deployment of short range SS-22 nuclear missiles in East Germany and Czechoslovakia — as the Soviet Union sought to put pressure on the Kohl government to shelve NATO modernisation plans. However, from the spring of 1984 both the East Germans — reacting to a power vacuum in Moscow following the death of Andropov and to its own desires for Western finance to meet its growing debt liabilities — and the Kohl government made steps towards a rapprochement, creating a small island of micro-detente in a troubled world of superpower conflict.

Thus, in June 1984 Bonn arranged, through the unlikely envoy of Franz-Josef Strauss, a large DM 1 billion loan to East Germany: in return, the East German government eased a number of its inter-German travel restrictions — exempting visitors below the age of 15 from compulsory exchange requirements and allowing a record number of East Germans (44 000) to leave the country to re-settle in the Federal Republic during 1984 — and handed control of the S-Bahn railway to West Berlin. Moscow later stepped in to pull East Germany into line and persuaded Erich Honecker to call off his much publicised and historic first official visit to West Germany in September 1984. A resumption in top level contacts between West Germany and Eastern European governments — including the Soviet Union, Poland and East Germany — during the winter of 1984 suggested that relations with the East were beginning to thaw once more. However, the eruption of the Tiedge spy scandal (August 1985) and the coming to power of the new Gorbachev administration in the Soviet Union, which was keen to re-establish firm control over its East European partners, dampened these hopes during 1985–6. Relations with East Germany particularly deteriorated during the summer and autumn of 1986 as a result of West German concern over the mounting influx of Third World 'economic refugees' through the 'Berlin hole' (see p. 95) and East Germany's anger at Chancellor Kohl's critical remarks on human rights within its borders (see p.71).[1] In addition, during 1985-6 the new Soviet leadership targetted the opposition SPD as a potential future ally in its drive to remove American nuclear weapons from Western Europe and destabilise the NATO alliance and thus sought to boost the SPD's prospects of gaining federal power in the January 1987 Bundestag election by giving it preferential treatment. A string of SPD officials, including party chairman Willy Brandt (September 1985), were thus invited to East Germany for top-level talks during 1985–6 and chemical weapons and nuclear-free zone agreements were negotiated by the neighbouring socialist parties of Germany (see p. 66). This strategy failed, however, in securing the SPD's election to power in January 1987. With the CDU-CSU-FDP Kohl administration set to govern for a further four year term and foreign minister Hans-Dietrich Genscher anxious to promote a new 'second phase of detente', an improvement in relations with the Soviet Union and East Germany thus appears likely to occur between 1987–90, as each side adjusts to the new realities of power.

West Germany's relations with its American ally have more perceptibly and steadily improved under the Kohl administration. The West German government has, however, displayed alarm at a number of the more adventurist initiatives of President Reagan,

[1] In consequence of this deterioration in relations, only 25 000 East Germans were allowed to leave and re-settle in West Germany during 1985 and only 20 000 during 1986.

particularly his policy in Lebanon and Libya, and has been divided over the American 'Star Wars' programme. Such doubts have served to push the West German government closer to its French allies within the European Community, and have raised interest in the development of a more concerted and co-ordinated EEC foreign and defence policy programme as a counterweight to the rival superpowers.

## West Germany in Europe and the developing world

The European Community has provided, in addition to a huge open market on West Germany's doorstep, a respectable route back to the international stage, though only during recent years has the voice of the EEC acquired strength and unity. All the major political parties in West Germany have, since 1959, been committed to the European ideal and this has been backed up by the West German government financially underwriting each new step in the Community's programme of development. It was not, however, until the early 1970s, based around the close co-operation of France and Germany, that major advances were made in achieving greater economic and governmental co-ordination and a political voice was successfully added to what had hitherto existed merely as a customs union and agricultural support service.

Under Helmut Schmidt and the French President, Valery Giscard d'Estaing, whose careers as national ministers and later leaders coincided between 1972 and 1981, the traditional hostility of France and Germany, which had still smouldered on during the Brandt-Pompidou era, at last gave way. A close rapprochement developed, born out of the mutual respect and affection of the two new leaders and out of a growing identity of interests.

West Germany, though possessing the largest and most powerful economy in Europe, remained wary, as a consequence of its past history, of playing a direct and overt role on the international stage. Having renounced the development of its own nuclear force and the stationing of German forces outside its frontiers, it lacked, in addition, the military might to perform such a role. However, Helmut Schmidt, the new German Chancellor, was very much an internationalist with a broad vision and a desire to leave his imprint on world politics. West Germany thus sought to work with and through the French government, led by an equally ambitious and confident leader, to achieve a number of its international aims. Contacts between the two countries' leaders, by telephone and bilateral summits, were frequent and economic policies converged, as Giscard d'Estaing, impressed with the postwar German 'economic miracle', sought to transpose the 'German model' into a French setting. In the European Community, the establishment of tri-annual 'European Council', co-ordinating meetings and an elected European Parliament, and the creation of the European Monetary System (EMS) in 1979 — set up to insulate European currencies against fluctuations in the US dollar — were significant policy developments in which the German input was immense, although much of the credit was allowed to pass to the French government. Outside Europe, West Germany worked with and through France to foster stability and peace in mineral-rich Africa and the Middle East.

With the fall of first Giscard d'Estaing in June 1981 and then Helmut Schmidt in October 1982, to be replaced respectively by the Socialist leader, Francois Mitterrand, and by the CDU leader, Helmut Kohl, the future of the firm Paris-Bonn axis was placed in question. France's new leader sought out alternative allies in Britain and Italy, while his reflationary domestic policies threatened to undermine the new EMS. The overtures to Britain and Italy failed, however, to elicit a reciprocal response, while Mitterrand's economic policy was soon subject to a deflationary U-turn. The Franco-German entente thus remained firmly in place during the years between 1983 and 1986, the major difference being that under the insular Helmut Kohl, the initiative for reform passed increasingly towards France.

The most important such initiative was Francois Mitterrand's drive for a more united and independent European defensive strategy, with close co-operation between the French army and the Bundeswehr and the development of the Eureka programme as an alternative or supplementary to US 'Star Wars' research, representing first steps in this direction.

This was partly stimulated by French anxiety concerning a possible dangerous drift towards Central European neutralism, which they saw developing in neighbouring Germany.

The West Germans under Helmut Kohl and Hans-Dietrich Genscher have, by contrast, placed particular emphasis on more rapid moves towards closer economic and political union within the Community and towards expediting the EEC entry of Spain and Portugal — smoothing over financial disputes between France and its Mediterranean neighbours through pecuniary subsidies. The strength of the West German farm lobby (particularly in the FDP,

CDU and CSU) and friendship with France has prevented West Germany, however, from pushing firmly for reform of the costly Common Agricultural Policy (CAP). Thus, as in Eastern Europe, West Germany has had to pay a significant economic price for diplomatic advances gained under the European and French umbrella.

Outside of Europe, West German direct actions have remained limited to economic matters, gaining, through its sheer economic weight, a seat at Western summits, which, as Helmut Schmidt demonstrated in 1978, could be used in a most effective and dramatic manner. West Germany's concern in other areas has been to promote stability and ease tensions between the superpower blocks. Such a concern reflects the twin economic and political imperatives for a country so heavily dependent on external trade and with its old capital Berlin cut in half and standing inside a hostile region, dependent upon the goodwill of its Eastern neighbour and the security provided by its Western allies.

# APPENDIX A

## The Länder (States) of the Federal Republic of Germany in July 1987

| | Area (Sq Km) | Population (1983) | Capital | Land Government | Bund-esrat Seats | % Religion Cath-olic | % Religion Pro-estant |
|---|---|---|---|---|---|---|---|
| Baden-Württemberg | 35 751 | 9 248 800 | Stuttgart | CDU | 5 | 47 | 46 |
| Bavaria | 70 552 | 10 965 800 | Munich | CSU | 5 | 70 | 26 |
| Bremen | 404 | 671 600 | Bremen | SPD | 3 | 10 | 82 |
| Hamburg | 755 | 1 600 300 | Hamburg | SPD-FDP | 3 | 8 | 74 |
| Hesse | 21 115 | 5 548 700 | Wiesbaden | CDU-FDP | 4 | 33 | 61 |
| Lower Saxony | 47 447 | 7 229 700 | Hanover | CDU-FDP | 5 | 20 | 75 |
| North-Rhine-Westphalia | 34 061 | 16 775 900 | Düsseldorf | SPD | 5 | 53 | 42 |
| Rhineland-Palatinate | 19 848 | 3 627 800 | Mainz | CDU-FDP | 4 | 56 | 41 |
| Saarland | 2 571 | 1 051 600 | Saarbrücken | SPD | 3 | 74 | 24 |
| Schleswig-Holstein | 15 721 | 2 615 100 | Kiel | CDU | 4 | 6 | 86 |
| West Berlin | 480 | 1 851 800 | West Berlin | CDU-FDP | 4[1] | 11 | 72 |
| Federal Total | 248 706 | 61 181 100 | Bonn | CDU-CSU-FDP | 45 | 45 | 47 |

[1] Non-voting

# APPENDIX B

## Länder Election Results: 1974-1987 (% of vote)

| | CDU | SPD | FDP | GREENS |
|---|---|---|---|---|
| BADEN-WURTTEMBERG | | | | |
| 1976 | 56.7 | 33.3 | 7.8 | — |
| 1980 | 53.4 | 32.5 | 8.3 | 5.3 |
| 1984 | 51.9 | 32.4 | 7.2 | 8.3 |
| | CDU Controlled | | | |
| BAVARIA | CSU | | | |
| 1974 | 62.1 | 30.2 | 5.2 | — |
| 1978 | 59.1 | 31.4 | 6.2 | 1.8 |
| 1982 | 58.3 | 31.9 | 3.5 | 4.6 |
| 1986[1] | 55.8 | 27.5 | 3.8 | 7.5 |
| | CSU Controlled | | | |

| | CDU | SPD | FDP | GREENS |
|---|---|---|---|---|
| BREMEN | CDU | | | |
| 1975 | 33.8 | 48.7 | 13.0 | — |
| 1979 | 31.9 | 49.4 | 10.8 | 5.1 |
| 1983 | 33.1 | 51.3 | 4.6 | 5.4[2] |

SPD Controlled

| | CDU | SPD | FDP | GREENS |
|---|---|---|---|---|
| HAMBURG | | | | |
| 1974 | 40.6 | 44.9 | 10.9 | — |
| 1978 | 37.6 | 51.5 | 4.8 | 4.5 |
| 1982a | 43.2 | 42.8 | 4.8 | 7.7 |
| 1982b | 38.6 | 51.3 | 2.6 | 6.8 |
| 1986 | 41.9 | 41.8 | 4.8 | 10.4 |
| 1987 | 39.3 | 46.5 | 6.0 | 7.1 |

SPD-FDP Controlled

| | CDU | SPD | FDP | GREENS |
|---|---|---|---|---|
| HESSE | | | | |
| 1974 | 40.3 | 48.5 | 10.2 | — |
| 1978 | 46.0 | 44.3 | 6.6 | — |
| 1982 | 45.6 | 42.8 | 3.1 | 8.0 |
| 1983 | 39.4 | 46.2 | 7.6 | 5.9 |
| 1987 | 42.1 | 40.2 | 7.8 | 9.4 |

CDU-FDP Controlled

| | CDU | SPD | FDP | GREENS |
|---|---|---|---|---|
| LOWER SAXONY | | | | |
| 1974 | 48.8 | 43.1 | 7.0 | — |
| 1978 | 48.7 | 42.2 | 4.2 | 3.9 |
| 1982 | 50.7 | 36.5 | 5.9 | 6.5 |
| 1986 | 44.7 | 42.1 | 6.0 | 7.1 |

CDU-FDP Controlled

| | CDU | SPD | FDP | GREENS |
|---|---|---|---|---|
| N. RHINE WESTPHALIA | | | | |
| 1975 | 47.1 | 45.1 | 6.7 | — |
| 1980 | 43.2 | 48.4 | 4.9 | 3.0 |
| 1985 | 36.0 | 52.0 | 5.6 | 4.8 |

SPD Controlled

| | CDU | SPD | FDP | GREENS |
|---|---|---|---|---|
| RHINELAND-PALATINATE | | | | |
| 1975 | 53.9 | 38.5 | 5.6 | — |
| 1979 | 50.1 | 42.3 | 6.4 | — |
| 1983 | 51.9 | 39.6 | 3.5 | 4.5 |
| 1987 | 45.1 | 39.0 | 7.2 | 5.8 |

CDU-FDP Controlled

| | CDU | SPD | FDP | GREENS |
|---|---|---|---|---|
| SAARLAND | | | | |
| 1975 | 49.1 | 41.8 | 7.4 | — |
| 1980 | 44.0 | 45.4 | 6.9 | 2.9 |
| 1985 | 37.0 | 49.0 | 10.0 | 2.5 |

SPD Controlled

| | CDU | SPD | FDP | GREENS |
|---|---|---|---|---|
| SCHLESWIG-HOLSTEIN | | | | |
| 1975 | 50.4 | 40.1 | 7.1 | — |
| 1979 | 48.3 | 41.7 | 5.8 | 2.4 |
| 1983 | 49.0 | 43.7 | 2.2 | 3.6 |

CDU Controlled

| | CDU | SPD | FDP | GREENS |
|---|---|---|---|---|
| WEST BERLIN | | | | |
| 1975 | 44.0 | 42.7 | 7.2 | — |
| 1979 | 44.4 | 42.6 | 8.1 | — |
| 1981 | 47.9 | 38.4 | 5.6 | 7.2 |
| 1985 | 46.0 | 32.0 | 8.4 | 10.6 |

CDU-FDP Controlled

[1]The rightwing Republicans (a breakaway from the CSU) captured 3% of the vote.

[2]The Bremen Green List also won 2.4%.

### EUROPEAN PARLIAMENT ELECTIONS
(% of Vote)

| | CDU-CSU | SPD | FDP | GREENS | TURNOUT |
|---|---|---|---|---|---|
| 1979 | 49.2 | 40.8 | 6.0 | 3.2 | (66%) |
| 1984 | 46.0 | 37.0 | 4.9 | 8.0 | (57%) |

# APPENDIX C

## Contemporary Länder Parliaments and Minister-Presidents

### Baden-Württemberg Landtag

(Seats after March 1984 election)

| CDU | SPD | GREENS | FDP |
|---|---|---|---|
| 68 | 41 | 9 | 8 |

MINISTER-PRESIDENT: Dr Lothar Späth (CDU) since August 1978

## Bavaria Landtag

(Seats after October 1986 election)

| CSU | SPD | GREENS |
|:---:|:---:|:---:|
| 128 | 61 | 15 |

MINISTER-PRESIDENT: Franz-Josef Strauss (CSU) since November 1978

## Bremen Senate (Bürgerschaft)

(Seats after September 1983 election)

| CDU | SPD | GREENS |
|:---:|:---:|:---:|
| 37 | 58 | 5 |

MAYOR (BÜRGERMEISTER): Klaus Wedemeier (SPD) since September 1985

## Hamburg Senate (Bürgershaft)

(Seats after May 1987 election)

| CDU | SPD | GREENS | FDP |
|:---:|:---:|:---:|:---:|
| 48 | 56 | 9 | 7 |

MAYOR (BURGERMEISTER): Dr Klaus Von Dohnanyi (SPD) since June 1981

## Hesse Landtag

(seats after April 1987 election)

| CDU | SPD | GREENS | FDP |
|:---:|:---:|:---:|:---:|
| 47 | 44 | 10 | 9 |

MINISTER PRESIDENT: Walter Wallmann (CDU) since April 1987

## Lower Saxony Landtag

(Seats after June 1986 election)

| CDU | SPD | GREENS | FDP |
|:---:|:---:|:---:|:---:|
| 69 | 66 | 11 | 9 |

MINISTER-PRESIDENT: Dr Ernst Albrecht (CDU) since December 1976

### North-Rhine-Westphalia Landtag

(Seats after May 1985 election)

| CDU | SPD | FDP |
|-----|-----|-----|
| 88 | 125 | 14 |

MINISTER-PRESIDENT: Johannes Rau (SPD) since September 1978

### Rhineland-Palatinate Landtag

(Seats after May 1987 election)

| CDU | SPD | GREENS | FDP |
|-----|-----|--------|-----|
| 47 | 40 | 6 | 7 |

MINISTER-PRESIDENT: Dr Bernhard Vogel (CDU) since October 1976

### Saarland Landtag

(Seats after March 1985 election)

| CDU | SPD | FDP |
|-----|-----|-----|
| 19 | 27 | 5 |

MINISTER-PRESIDENT: Oskar Lafontaine (SPD) since March 1985

### Schleswig-Holstein Landtag

(Seats after March 1983 election)

| CDU | SPD | SW* |
|-----|-----|-----|
| 39 | 34 | 1 |

*Sudschleswigscher Wahlerverband

MINISTER-PRESIDENT: Dr Uwe Barschel (CDU) since October 1982

## The Positions of the Parties in West Germany's 11 Landtage in July 1987[1]

|  | Seats | Number of Landtage under Full Control | Number of Landtage under Shared Control | Bundesrat Seats |
|--|-------|---------------------------------------|------------------------------------------|-----------------|
| CDU-CSU | 659 | 3 | 4 | 31[2] |
| SPD | 600 | 3 | 1 | 14 |
| Greens[3] | 80 | — | — | — |
| FDP | 71 | — | 5 | — |

[1]Including West Berlin
[2]Including four non-voting West Berlin delegates
[3]Including the 'Alternative List' in West Berlin

## APPENDIX D

### The Constitutional Position of West Berlin

West Berlin, although classed in the Basic Law as a Land of the Federal Republic, remains subject to the supreme authority of the three Allied powers of the United States, Britain and France in accordance with postwar agreements. This ambiguous status was confirmed by the June 1972 Four Power Agreement in which the three Allied nations agreed that West Berlin was not a constituent part of the FGR, while the Soviet Union confirmed the Allied troika's governing rights.

Under the Land's August 1950 constitution, West Berlin has a single chamber, popularly elected 133-member legislature, the House of Representatives (*Abgeordnetenhaus*). The House elects a 10-16 member executive, termed the Senate and a Governing Mayor (*Regierender Bürgermeister*) to run the city's affairs. In addition, it appoints four delegates to the Federal Bundesrat and 22 'honorary delegates' to the Bundestag who are debarred from voting in plenary sessions. The latter delegates are selected on a proportionate basis so as to accurately reflect the balance of party strength within the House.

### House of Representatives

(Following the March 1985 election)

|  | % of Votes | Seats |
|---|---|---|
| CDU | 46 | 69 |
| SPD | 32 | 48 |
| Alternative List (Green) | 11 | 15 |
| FDP | 8 | 12 |

GOVERNING MAYOR: Eberhard Diepgen (CDU) since May 1984

## APPENDIX E

### West Germany's Political Parties — Membership and Organisation

#### Party Membership: 1950-1985

('000)

|  | 1950 | 1960 | 1970 | 1980 | 1985 |
|---|---|---|---|---|---|
| SPD | 683 | 650 | 780 | 980 | 930 |
| CDU | 265 | 270 | 300 | 696 | 736 |
| CSU | 90 | — | 118 | 175 | 186 |
| FDP | 80 | — | 58 | 85 | 80 |
| GREENS | — | — | — | 19 | 40 |
| DKP | — | — | 22 | 45 | 49 |
| NPD | — | — | — | 10 | 15 |
| Republicans | — | — | — | — | 4 |

## Social Democratic Party (SPD)
*(Sozialdemokratische Partei Deutschlands)*

Date of Formation: 1875

Chairman: Hans-Jöchen Vogel (since 1987)
Deputy Chairmen: Johannes Rau (since 1982), Oskar Lafontaine (since 1987)
Bundestag Leader: Hans-Jöchen Vogel (since 1983)

Organisational Structure
The SPD is the most centralised and tightly organised of the major parties in West Germany. The party congress is held every two years and elects a policy making 42-member National Executive Committee. The Executive Committee is dominated by an inner 9-member Presidium which includes the party's chairman, deputy chairmen and Bundestag Fraktion leader. Executive Committees similarly function at the Länder level, often displaying considerable autonomy from the federal party headquarters. The party also possesses influential 'youth' (Jusos) and trade union wings.

Party Finance
Total Income in the election year of 1980, Dm 207 million, of which 24% was derived from the state in reimbursement for its campaign expenses, 34% from membership fees, 8% from the parliamentary party and 6% came from donations.

## Free Democratic Party (FDP)
*(Freie Demokratische Partei Deutschlands)*

Date of Formation: 1948

Chairman: Martin Bangemann (since 1985)
Bundestag Leader: Wolfgang Mischnick
Secretary-General: Helmut Haussmann

Organisational Structure
A 400-member federal FDP Congress meets annually and elects a national committee and federal executive, headed by the party chairman, at two-yearly intervals. Länder FDP organisations retain, however, considerable independence.

Party Finance
Total income in 1980, Dm 35 million: 33% from the state, 14% from membership fees, 6% from the parliamentary party, 31% from donations.

## Christian Democratic Union (CDU)
### (*Christlich-Demokratische Union*)

Date of Formation: 1945

Chairman: Dr Helmut Kohl (since 1973)
Bundestag Leader: Alfred Dregger
Secretary-General: Dr Heiner Geissler

Organisational Structure
The party, having been formed as a 'Union' of regional conservative groupings, is necessarily decentralised in structure. Biannual congresses are held in each Land to elect executive committees which select Bundestag candidates and frame local policies. A national Congress of 800 delegates chosen by Länder officials meets annually to elect, for a two-year term, a 60-member Executive Committee headed by the party Chairman. The party also possesses important youth and business wings.

Party Finance
Total income in 1980, Dm 176 million; 22% from the state, 28% from membership fees, 8% from the parliamentary party, 27% from donations.

## Christian Social Union (CSU)
### (*Christlich-Soziale Union*)

Date of Formation: 1946

Chairman: Dr Franz-Josef Strauss (since 1961)
Bundestag Leader: Theo Waigel
Secretary-General: Gerold Tandler

Organisational Structure
The party, which is based solely in Bavaria, forms a joint Bundestag Fraktion with the CDU and supports a commonly agreed chancellor-candidate in federal Bundestag elections. Franz-Josef Strauss, chairman since 1961, dominates party policy making, although there exist 2,900 local associations which retain considerable autonomy.

Party Finance
Total income in 1980, Dm 45 million: 17% from the state, 19% from membership fees, 8% from the parliamentary party, 36% from donations.

## Green Party
### (*Die Grünen*)

Date of Formation: 1980

Troika Executive: Rainer Trampert, Lukas Beckmann, Jutta Ditfurth.
Parliamentary Leadership: Sextumvirate led by Hannegret Hönes.

Organisational Structure
The party, having been formed by bringing together a group of regionally based environmental pressure groups, is unusually decentralised in structure. National congresses are, however, held annually to elect a 17-member National Executive Committee which is composed of representatives from all Länder. The party has a unique collective form of national and parliamentary leadership and regularly rotates leadership functions. addition, the party's statutes require that women be equally represented at all executive levels.

## German Communist Party (DKP)*
### (*Deutsche Kommunistische Partei*)

Date of Formation: 1968

Chairman: Herbert Mies

Organisational Structure
Organised on strict, communist 'democratic centralist' lines with a Politburo and Central Committee 'elected' by a national Congress. The party enjoys considerable financial support from sources within East Germany.

Party Finance
Total income in 1980, Dm 13 million: 2% from the state, 16% from membership fees, 4% from the parliamentary party, 38% from donations.

*An earlier version of this party, the KPD (*Kommunistische Partei Deutschlands*), which had been formed in 1918, was banned in 1956.

## German National Party (NPD)
### (*Nationaldemokratische Partei Deutschlands*)

Date of Formation: 1964

Chairman: Martin Mussgnug

Party Finance
In 1980 53% of party funds were derived from donations and 33% from membership fees.

**Republican Party**
(*Republikaner Partei*)

Date of Formation: 1984

Chairman: Franz Schonhüber

## APPENDIX F

## The West German Newspaper and Television Media

The pattern of newspaper circulation in West Germany is intermediate between the high volume, relatively concentrated national pattern to be found in Great Britain and the diffuse, regionally based pattern of neighbouring France. In Britain total national daily newspaper circulation amounted in 1986 to 15.5 million copies, with six major popular, national tabloids — *The Sun* (circulation 4.1 million), the *Daily Mirror* (3 million), *Daily Express* (1.9 million), *Daily Mail* (1.8 million), *The Star* (1.5 million) and, the recent addition, *Today* — accounting for 84% of sales, with five serious, national 'quality' newspapers — the *Daily Telegraph* (1.1 million) *The Times* (0.48 million), *The Guardian* (0.49 million), *Financial Times* (0.23 million) and *The Independent* (0.3 million) accounting for the remaining 16%. The only major morning newspapers with a regional distribution are the Scottish *Daily Record* (0.76 million) and *Glasgow Herald* (0.12 million). The remainder of the provincial press consists of either evening (circulation 6 million) or weekly newspapers. In France, by contrast, where daily newspaper circulation averages 11.3 million copies, 73 medium-sized provincial dailies are responsible for two-thirds of total sales, while the eleven nationally orientated newspapers published in Paris have combined sales of only 3.8 million copies, averaging circulations of only 100 000-400 000 copies apiece.

In West Germany total daily circulation, which presently stands at more than 21 million copies, is among the highest in Europe, with the national tabloid, *Bild Zeitung* (circulation 5.4 million) standing at the top of the European daily newspaper league. There are, in addition, a clutch of four nationally orientated 'quality' daily newspapers — the conservative *Die Welt* (0.2 million) and *Frankfurter Allgemeine Zeitung* (0.35 million), the liberal *Süddeutsche Zeitung* (0.35 million) and the left-of-centre Frankfurter *Rundschau* (0.2 million) — with a combined circulation exceeding one million. The remainder of the West German press is, however, as in France, regionally based as the table below displays. In addition, as a consequence of the relative weakness of the national daily and Sunday press, the sales of weekly current affairs magazines are far higher in West

Germany (as in France) than in Britain. In Britain, *The Economist*, with sales of 0.26 million, is the only significant weekly. In West Germany, the liberal *Die Zeit* (0.4 million) and *Der Spiegel* (0.9 million) are unusually influential journals. Finally, a significant share of newspaper circulation is in the hands of a few major combines, the most significant being the conservative, Hamburg, West Berlin and Bonn based Springer press.

The radio and television medium in West Germany is under the control of nine, non-profitmaking public corporations based at the Land level (Hamburg, Lower Saxony and Schleswig-Holstein having a combined service) and originally organised during the 1945-9 period of occupation. Each corporation is governed by a broadcasting council consisting of a balanced mixture of representatives from all the major 'social, economic, cultural and political forces'. The corporations are financed predominantly through monthly license fees paid by owners of radio and television receivers and partially by advertising. There are three television channels: on Channel 1 the nine regional broadcasting corporations combine to provide material under the direction of the central ARD (*Arbeitsgemein-schaft der öffentlich-rechtlichen Rundfunkanstalten der Bundesrepublik Deutschland*); Channel 2 (established in 1964 and partly funded by advertising) is completely in the hands of the local Land corporations who have formed a joint corporation, the ZDF (*Zweites Deutsches Fernsehen*), based in Mainz, to oversee programming; Channel 3, which only transmits in the evening, concentrates on cultural and educational programmes, with contributions from several of the regional bodies.

## National and Provincial Daily Newspaper Circulation
(Papers with Circulations of 100 000 or more)

| NEWSPAPER TITLE | PLACE OF PUBLICATION | REGION | CIRCULATION |
|---|---|---|---|
| Aachener Volkszeitung | Aachen | N-Central | 106 000 |
| Abendzeitung/8-Uhr-Blatt | Munich | South | 270 000 |
| Allgäuer Zeitung | Kempten | South | 110 000 |
| Allgemeine Zeitung | Mainz | Central | 128 000 |
| Augsburger Allgemeine | Augsburg | South | 340 000 |
| Badische Neueste Nachrichten | Karlsruhe | South | 167 000 |
| Badische Zeitung | Freiburg | South | 170 000 |
| Berliner Morgenpost | West Berlin | East | 180 000[1] |
| Berliner Zeitung | West Berlin | East | 307 000[1] |
| Bild Zeitung | Hamburg | National | 5 400 000[1] |
| Braunschweiger Zeitung | Brunswick | North | 167 000 |
| Der Targesspiegel | West Berlin | East | 120 000 |
| Die Rheinpfalz | Ludwigshafen | Central | 240 000 |
| Die Welt | Bonn | National | 200 000[1] |
| Express | Cologne | N-Central | 450 000 |
| Frankfurter Allgemeine Zeitung | Frankfurt | National | 350 000 |
| Frankfurter Neue Presse | Frankfurt | Central | 129 000 |

137

| NEWSPAPER TITLE | PLACE OF PUBLICATION | REGION | CIRCULATION |
|---|---|---|---|
| Frankfurter Rundschau | Frankfurt | National | 196 000 |
| Hamburger Abendblatt | Hamburg | North | 280 000[1] |
| Hamburger Morgenpost | Hamburg | North | 236 000 |
| Hannoversche Allgemeine Zeitung | Hanover | North | 208 000 |
| Heilbroner Stimme | Heilbronn | South | 104 000 |
| Hessische Allgemeine | Kassel | N-Central | 230 000 |
| Kieler Nachrichten | Kiel | North | 112 000 |
| Kölner Stadt-Anzeiger | Cologne | N-Central | 263 000 |
| Kölnische Rundschau | Cologne | N-Central | 160 000 |
| Lübecker Nachrichten | Lübeck | North | 112 000 |
| Main-Post | Würzburg-Heuchelhof | South | 155 000 |
| Mannheimer Morgen | Mannheim | South | 184 000 |
| Mittelbayerische Zeitung | Regensburg | South | 100 000 |
| Münchner Merkur | Munich | South | 167 000 |
| Neue Osnabrücker Zeitung | Osnabrück | North | 183 000 |
| Neue Ruhr Zeitung | Essen | N-Central | 215 000 |
| Neue Westfälische | Bielefeld | N-Central | 209 000 |
| Nordwest-Zeitung | Oldenburg | North | 116 000 |
| Nürnberger Nachrichten | Nuremberg | South | 340 000 |
| Passauer Neue Presse | Passau | South | 145 000 |
| Rheinische Post | Düsseldorf | N-Central | 395 000 |
| Rhein-Neckar-Zeitung | Heidelberg | Central | 100 000 |
| Rhein-Zeitung | Koblenz | Central | 223 000 |
| Ruhr-Nachrichten | Dortmund | N-Central | 253 000 |
| Saarbrücker Zeitung | Saarbrücken | Central | 205 000 |
| Schwäbische Zeitung | Leutkirch | South | 190 000 |
| Stuttgarter Nachrichten | Stuttgart | South | 260 000 |
| Stuttgarter Zeitung | Stuttgart | South | 163 000 |
| Süddeutchsche Zeitung | Munich | National | 350 000 |
| Südkurier | Konstanz | South | 137 000 |
| Südwest Presse | Ulm | South | 356 000 |
| Weser-Kurier | Bremen | North | 185 000 |
| Westdeutsche Allgemeine Zeitung | Essen | N-Central | 660 000 |
| Westdeutsche Zeitung | Düsseldorf | N-Central | 216 000 |
| Westfalen-Blatt | Bielefeld | N-Central | 147 000 |
| Westfalenpost | Hagen | N-Central | 155 000 |
| Westfälische Nachrichten | Münster | N-Central | 202 000 |
| Westfälische Rundschau | Dortmund | N-Central | 245 000 |

## Sunday and Weekly Newspapers

| TITLE | PLACE OF PUBLICATION | CIRCULATION |
|---|---|---|
| Bild am Sonntag | Hamburg | 2 400 000[1] |
| Deutsches Allgemeines Sonntagsblatt | Hamburg | 129 000 |
| Welt am Sonntag | Hamburg | 336 000[1] |

## Weekly Magazines

| TITLE | PLACE OF PUBLICATION | CIRCULATION |
|---|---|---|
| Bayernkurier | Munich | 170 000[2] |
| Der Spiegel | Hamburg | 915 000 |
| Die Zeit | Hamburg | 398 000 |
| Neue Post | Hamburg | 1 995 000 |
| Neue Revue | Hamburg | 1 250 000 |
| Neue Welt | Düsseldorf | 445 000 |
| Rheinischer Merkur | Koblenz | 133 000 |
| Stern | Hamburg | 1 525 000 |
| Vorwärts | Bonn | 65 000[3] |

[1] Part of Springer group
[2] The organ of the CSU
[3] The organ of the SPD

## ABBREVIATIONS, GLOSSARY OF GERMAN TERMS AND
## ADDITIONAL BIOGRAPHICAL INFORMATION

**Adenauer, Konrad** (1876–1967) — Chancellor 1949–63 and dominating figure in West German politics and the CDU during the first decade of the Fourth Reich. Born into a lower middle class Cologne family, he trained as a lawyer and served as a 'Centre Party' mayor of Cologne (1917–33) during the Weimar period. He gained a reputation as a firm opponent of Nazism during the 1930s.

**APO** (Ausserparlamentarische Opposition) — The controlling body behind the student protest movement of the mid and late 1960s.

**BDA** (Bundesvereinigung der Deutschen Arbeitgeberverbände) — Confederation of German Employers' Associations: President Otto Esser. The BDA is particularly concerned with social questions and industrial relations issues affecting employers.

**BDI** (Bundesvereinigung der Deutschen Industrie) — Confederation of German Industry. The BDI is closely linked to the BDA and concentrates on economic issues of concern to industrialists.

**Beamte** (pl.-n) — Career civil-servant with special privileges and responsibilities.

**Berufsverbot** ('Professional Ban') — Job-vetting rules for public service introduced in 1972 to exclude members of anti-constitutional groupings.

**BFV** (Bundesamt für Verfassungsschutz: Office for the Protection of the Constitution) — Internal counter-intelligence agency.

**BHE** (Block der Heimatvertriebenen und Entrechteten: 'League of those expelled from their homeland and deprived of their rights') — Expellees Party formed in 1950. It gradually lost support to and was absorbed by the CDU during the 1950s.

**BND** (Bundesnachrichtendienst) — Federal Counter-Intelligence Service. Concerned with foreign espionage.

**Brandt, Willy** (1913– ) — Born Herbert Ernst Karl Frahm, the illegitimate son of a Lübeck shopgirl, he joined the SPD at the age of 16 in 1929 and became an active opponent of Nazism. During the Third Reich era he was forced into exile in Norway, where he changed his name and became a resistance leader. He returned to Germany after the war and based himself in West Berlin, becoming its mayor in 1957 and holding office during the 1958 airlift and 1961 Berlin wall crises. Brandt was appointed chairman of the SPD in 1964 (holding the post till 1987) and served as foreign minister during the 1966–9 'Grand Coalition' and as Chancellor between 1969–72, establishing the reputation as the architect of Ospolitik.

**Bund** (pl-e) — Federation

**Bundesrat** — Upper chamber of Federal parliament composed of 41 full voting representatives drawn from Länder governments and 4 non-voting representatives from West Berlin.

**Bundestag** — Lower, popularly elected, chamber of federal parliament (Diet). It is composed of at least 496 full voting representatives and 22 'honorary deputies' from West Berlin.

**Bundesverfassungsgericht** — Federal Constitutional Court. An independent 16-member constitutional watchdog.

**Bundesversammlung** — Federal convention composed of Bundestag deputies and an equal number of Landtage representatives which is specially convened to elect the Federal President.

**Bundeswehr** — Federal German army.

**Bürgerinitiative** (pl.-n) — Citizens' Initiative Group (Local Pressure Group)

**Bürgermeister** — City mayor.

**Bürgerschaft** — City parliament.

**CAP** — Common Agriculture Policy of the EEC, involving a system of price subsidies to maintain agricultural production.

**CDU** — Christian Democratic Union.

**CSU** — Christian Social Union.

**Deutsche Mark** — West German currency unit. In 1976 there were 2.52 DM per US $, in 1980, 1.82, and in 1986, 2.0, with 2.9 DM per £.

**DGB** (Deutsche Gewerkschaftsbund) — West German trade union confederation: total membership 7.6 million, President Ernst Breit.

**DKP** — German Communist Party (since 1968).

**DP** (Deutsche Partei) — German Party. A conservative party drawing strong support from Protestants in Lower Saxony and Bremen during the 1950s. It was gradually absorbed by the CDU.

**ECU** — European Currency Unit.

**EEC** — European Economic Community. Formed following March 1957 Treaty of Rome.

**EMS** — European Monetary System of fixed exchange rates. Established in 1979.

**Erhard, Ludwig** (1897-1977) — Chancellor 1963-6 and finance minister 1949-63, he was the architect of the postwar West

German 'economic miracle'. The son of a North Bavarian Catholic farmer turned haberdasher and a Protestant mother, he was brought up as a Protestant and, after studying economics at Nuremberg's Handelshochschule, worked in the Institute of Market Research during the interwar period. His career was held back during the 1930s by his refusal to join the local Nazi party, but took off during the 1945−49 American occupation era when he was placed in charge of financial planning for the Frankfurt economic council. He resigned as Chancellor in 1966 when his party and coalition colleagues refused to support his proposal to increase taxes at a time of economic difficulty.

**Erststimme** (pl-n) — First vote cast at elections which is used to elect consituency members on a first-past-the-post basis.

**FDP** — Free Democratic Party

**Finanzausgleich** — System of adjusting the tax shares given to each state to take account of population and social needs.

**Finanzplanungsrat** — Financial Planning Council, which helps co-ordinate economic activity at the federal and Lander level.

**First Reich** — 768−911 AD Carolingian Empire.

**Fourth Reich** — The postwar West German Federal Republic.

**Fraktion** (pl.−en) — Party caucus of at least 25 members within the Bundestag on which basis committee seats and chairs are assigned.

**FRG** — Federal Republic of Germany (West Germany).

**GAL** — Green Alternative List. Lists put up by environmentalists in a number of Länder.

**Gastarbeiter** — Foreign workers brought in from southern Europe during the 1950s and 1960s 'miracle years'.

**GAZ** (Grüne Aktion Zukunft) — Moderate environmentalist party led by Herbert Gruhl and based in Baden-Württemberg.

**GDR** — German Democratic Republic (East Germany).

**Gemeinde** (pl. −n) — Municipality.

**Genscher,** Hans-Dietrich (1927−   ) — Born in Halle, which is today in East Germany, Genscher settled in the Federal Republic in 1952 and became a leading member of the FDP. He was elected a Bundestag deputy in 1960 and served as federal interior minister between 1969−74, before being appointed Vice-Chancellor and foreign minister in 1974: posts he has held ever since. Genscher was chairman of the FDP between 1974−85 and remains an influential party strategist. He is a committed supporter of Ostpolitik detente.

**Grundgesetz** — The 1949 'Basic Law' constitution of the Federal Republic.

**Guillaume, Günter** — A former East German Army officer, Guillaume came to the Federal Republic in 1956 as a 'refugee', joined the SPD (1957) and worked his way up to become a close aide to Willy Brandt in the Federal Chancellery, handling secret and sensitive documents. His unmasking as an East German spy in April 1974 forced the resignation of Willy Brandt as Chancellor in May 1974.

**Heinemann, Gustav** (1899–1976) — President of the Federal Republic 1969–74. Originally a member of the CDU and minister of the interior in the first Adenauer cabinet of 1949, he resigned, being a pacifist, over the question of West German rearmament in 1950 and formed his own neutralist party, before later joining the SPD. He served as justice minister in the 1966–9 'Grand Coalition'.

**Honecker, Erich** (1912– ) — Leader of the ruling SED in East Germany since 1971. Having been born in the Saarland in East Germany, he has been a warm supporter of Ostpolitik.

**Judos** — Young Democrat section of FDP.

**Junker** — Large, estate-owning landlord during Second Reich era.

**Jusos** — Young Socialist section of the SPD.

**Kaiser** — German Emperor during the Second Reich.

**Kanalarbeiter** ('Channel Worker') — Member of moderate grouping, loyal to the leadership, within the SPD.

**Kiesinger, Kurt** (1904– ) Chancellor of the Federal Republic 1966-9. He was born near Stuttgart and was brought up as a Catholic (his father was a Protestant and his mother a Catholic). He trained as a lawyer and was a member, although not active, of the Nazi Party between 1933–45. After the war he joined the newly formed CDU and served as minister-president of his native Baden-Württemberg between 1958–66. He was a member of the Bundestag between 1949–58 and 1969–80, aligning himself to the liberal wing of the CDU.

**Konjunkturrat** — Counter-cyclical advisory council for economic development.

**Konzertierte Aktion** ('Concerted Action') — System of tripartite discussions between government, business and trade union leaders which sought, during the 1970s, to establish a framework within which wage bargaining and industrial investment decisions could be rationally made.

**KPD** — German Communist Party (1918—56). It was formed from the USPD.

**Kreis** (pl. —e) — District.

**Land** (pl. Länder) — Constituent state of the Federal Republic.

**Landtag** (pl. —e) — State assembly.

**Leverkusen Circle** — Leftist trade union and Jusos grouping within the SPD.

**Machtwechsel** — Changeover in political power.

**Mitbestimmung** — Industrial co-determination, involving the co-option of workers leaders on to boards of management.

**Mittelstand** (pl. stände) — Medium-sized, niche firms.

**NATO** — North Atlantic Treaty Organisation. The grouping of West European nations with the United States and Canada in April 1949 to work together to safeguard the security of Europe. West Germany joined the organisation in 1955.

**NICS** — Newly Industrialised Countries (particularly of SE Asia).

**Nordlichter** ('Northern light') — Term given to liberal, often Protestant, members of CDU based in northern Germany.

**NPD** — National Party of Germany (since 1964).

**Ostpolitik** ('Eastern policy') — Policy of improving relations with Eastern Europe launched by Brandt in 1966.

**Parteiengesetz** — 1967 Party Law regulating the position of parties and providing for partial state financing.

**Parteienstaat** ('Party State') — Term used to describe the Fourth Reich political system as a result of the privileged position given to political parties.

**PLO** — Palestine Liberation Organisation.

**PR** — Proportional Representation.

**Reichstag** — Elected federal parliamentary assembly during Second Reich and Weimar (1919—33) periods.

**Schiller, Karl** (1911—   ) A former, though non-active, member of the Nazi Party during the 1930s, he became an economics professor at Hamburg University after the war and served as a successful SPD minister of finance between 1966—72. He resigned in June 1972 as a result of policy differences with Chancellor Brandt.

**Second Reich** — 1871—1919 German Empire period.

**SED** — East German Communist Party.

**Soziale Marktwirtschaft** ('Social Market Economy') — Postwar system of capitalist/Christian Socialist form of economic management in the Federal Republic.

**Spartakus Revolution** — January 1919 uprising in Berlin by the

144

extreme left USPD which was crushed by moderate members of the SPD and military forces.

**SPD** — Social Democratic Party.

**SRP** (Sozialistische Reichspartei) — Far-right Socialist Reich Party which was banned in 1952.

**Staatssekretar** (pl. −e) — Chief civil-servant at the head of a ministry.

**Third Reich** — 1933−45 Nazi (National Socialist) period.

**Überhangmandat** (pl. −e) — Additional seat gained by a party winning more seats in a Land in constituency contests than was indicated by its overall List vote.

**USPD** (Unabhängige Socialdemokratische Partei Deutschlands) — Far-left breakaway grouping from SPD in 1917 which was the forerunner of the KPD.

**Vermittlungsausschuss** — Joint conciliation committee of Bundesrat and Bundestag representatives established to iron out differences over legislation.

**Volkspartei** (pl. −en) — A 'catch all' party drawing support from a wide range of social groupings.

**Wehner, Herbert** (1906−   ) Born in Dresden (East Germany), he joined the German Communist Party in 1927 and was forced into exile during the Nazi era. On his return to Germany in 1946, he joined the SPD in Hamburg and became party manager during the late 1950s. During the 1966−9 'Grand Coalition' he served as minister for inter-German affairs, emerging as a strong advocate of Ostpolitik detente, and between 1969−83 acted as the SPD's Bundestag Fraktion leader and as an influential party tactician.

**Wehrmacht** — German army during the Third Reich.

**Wende** — Political, economic and social turning point.

**Zollverein** — German free-trading union established during the Second Reich.

**Zweitstimme** (pl. −n) — Second vote at elections which is used to determine the number of seats a party will receive in each Land.

# RECENT BOOKS ON WEST GERMAN POLITICS

K. L. BAKER, R. J. DALTON and K. HILDEBRANDT (Eds.) — *Germany Transformed*: Political Culture and the New Politics (Cambridge, Mass.: Harvard University Press 1981).

M. BALFOUR — *West Germany*: A Contemporary History (London: Croom Helm 1982).

P. M. BLAIR — *Federalism and Judicial Review in West Germany* (Oxford: Clarendon Press 1981).

W. BRANDT — *People and Politics*: The Years 1960–1975 (London: Collins 1978).

C. BURDICK, H. A. JACOBSEN and W. KUDSZUS (Eds.) — *Contemporary Germany*: Politics and Culture (Epping: Bowker 1984).

J. CARR — *Helmut Schmidt*: Helmsman of Germany (London: Weidenfeld and Nicolson, 1985).

K. H. CERNY (Ed.) — *Germany at the Polls*: The Bundestag Election of 1976 (Washington D.C.: American Enterprise Institute 1978).

D. CHILDS and J. JOHNSON — *West Germany*: Politics and Society (London: Croom Helm 1981).

D. P. CONRADT — *The German Policy* (New York: Longman, 2nd edn. 1981).

L. J. EDINGER — *Politics in West Germany* (Boston: Little Brown 1977).

W. GRAF — *The German Left since 1945* (Cambridge: Oleander Press 1976).

W. E. GRIFFITHS — *The Ostpolitik of the Federal Republic of Germany* (Cambridge, Mass.: Harvard University Press 1978).

E. HARTRICH — *The Fourth and Richest Reich* (London: Macmillan 1980).

N. JOHNSON — *State and Government in the Federal Republic of Germany*: The Executive at Work (Oxford: Pergamon Press 1983, 2nd edn.)

M. KAASE and K. VON BEYME (Eds.) — *Elections and Parties*: Socio-Political Change in the West Germany Federal Election of 1976 (London: Sage 1978).

W. L. KOHL and G. BASEVI (Eds.) — *West Germany*: A European and Global Power (Lexington: Gower 1981).

E. KOLINSKY — *Parties, Opposition and Society in West Germany* (London: Croom Helm 1984).

R. F. NYROP (Ed) — *Federal Republic of Germany*: A Country Study (Washington D.C.: The American University 1982).

E. PAPADAKIS — *The Green Movement in West Germany* (London: Croom Helm 1984).

W. E. PATERSON and G. SMITH (Eds) — *The West German Model*: Perspectives on a Stable State (London: Cass 1981).

G. PRIDHAM — *Christian Democracy in Western Germany* (London: Croom Helm 1977).

T. PRITTIE — *The Velvet Chancellors*: A History of Post-War Germany (London: Muller 1979).

H. SIMONIAN — *The Privileged Partnership*: Franco-German Relations in the European Community, 1969–1984 (Oxford: Clarendon 1985).

146

G. SMITH — *Democracy in West Germany*: Parties and Politics in the Federal Republic (London: Heinemann, 2nd edn. 1982).

G. SMITH and H. DORING (Eds.) — *Party Government and Political Culture in Western Germany* (London: Macmillan 1982).

A. STENT — *From Embargo to Ostpolitik*: The Political Economy of West German-Soviet relations, 1955–1980 (Cambridge: Cambridge University Press 1981).

K. VON BEYME — *The Political System of the Federal Republic of Germany* (Aldershot: Gower 1983).

## CHRONOLOGY OF RECENT EVENTS: 1976–1987

**1976**      Oct, Bundestag elections, CDU-CSU, led by Helmut Kohl, gain 48.6% of vote, but SPD-FDP stay in power. Nov, Strauss's CSU temporarily break with CDU.

**1977**      Genesis of Green Party. Jan, Carter new US President. Sept, terrorist outrages peak with kidnap of Schleyer and Lufthansa hi-jack: firm Schmidt emerges as the 'hero of Mogadishu'.

**1978**      July, Bonn summit, Schmidt launches DM 13 billion reflation package. Nov, six week steel strike for 35-hour week.

**1979**      Jan, EMS begins operation. July, Strauss adopted as CDU-CSU chancellor-candidate. Oct, Greens gain first seats in a Landtag (Bremen). Nov, Iran-Iraq war leads to oil price hike. Dec, Soviet Union invade Afghanistan.

**1980**      Polish crisis. Oct, SPD-FDP coalition led by Helmut Schmidt and Hans-Dietrich Genscher win Bundestag election, CDU-CSU vote falls to 44.5%. Dec, new immigration controls.

**1981**      Jan, Reagan new US President. May, Mitterrand new French President. SPD lose in West Berlin stronghold. Dec, Chancellor Schmidt meets Erich Honecker in the GDR — martial law is declared in Poland. Unemployment soars to 1.7 million.

**1982**      Sept, Lambsdorff 'memorandum'. Oct, Kohl (CDU) with FDP support topples Schmidt and becomes Chancellor. Schmidt resigns as SPD leader to be replaced by Hans-Jöchen Vogel.

**1983**      March, CDU-CSU-FDP win Bundestag election. Greens win 27 seats. Oct, peace demonstrations. Nov, SPD conference opposes Pershing deployment, but Bundestag votes in favour. Kiessling and Flick scandals. New immigrant repatriation scheme.

**1984** May, seven week IG-Metall strike leads to 38½-hour week; Von Weizsäcker elected federal president. June, FDP fail to win seats in Euro-election; Greens win 8% of vote. Lambsdorff (FDP), and in Oct., Barzel (CDU) resign over 'Flick affair'.

**1985** Feb, Bangemann becomes FDP leader. March, Greens 'rotate' Bundestag deputies. May, SPD, led by Johannes Rau gain huge victory in North-Rhine-Westphalia. Sept, Tiedge spy scandal. Dec, Greens-SPD coalition formed in Hesse.

**1986** Unemployment begins to fall below 2.3 million. April, Chernobyl nuclear disaster in the Soviet Union. May, Kohl cleared of perjury. June, CDU retain control of Lower Saxony. Aug, Rau elected chancellor-candidate for the SPD. Sept, Neue Heimat affair. Oct/Nov, setback for SPD in Bavaria and Hamburg election: significant advances by the Greens, helped by Rhine river chemical disaster.

**1987** Jan., CDU-CSU-FDP coalition re-elected to power in Bundestag election: CDU-CSU and SPD vote falls, FDP and Greens gain substantial support. Feb, Flick trial ends: Lambsdorff cleared of bribery. March, New Kohl cabinet sworn in and tax reforming legislative programme proposed; resignation of Willy Brandt as SPD chairman. April, CDU-FDP defeat SPD in Hesse Land election.

## BRITAIN

FROM CALLAGHAN
TO THATCHER

The background to the Callaghan and Thatcher eras, from 1945-76; the Callaghan Administration 1976-79; the first Thatcher Administration 1979-83; the second Thatcher Administration 1983-87; the Thatcher Third Term from 1987.

---

## FRANCE

FROM GISCARD
TO MITTERRAND

Examines and explains the key changes in French politics over the most recent decade. Considers the varying fortunes of the major parties and ideological coalitions; changing policy directions; the dominant personalities. Looks in particular at the modernisation of the inherited Gaullist state and at the 1981-85 "Socialist Experiment" and the post-1986 "cohabitation" experience.

# CHAMBERS POLITICAL SPOTLIGHTS

POLITICS IN

## THE SOVIET UNION

FROM BREZHNEV
TO GORBACHEV

Political changes/defence
and foreign policies/
economic and social
developments/internal
opposition.

---

# CHAMBERS POLITICAL SPOTLIGHTS

POLITICS IN

## CHINA

FROM MAO
TO DENG

Examines the key changes in
the Chinese political and
economic system during the
years from 1972 to 1987.
Looks at the changing
functions of political
institutions, at the
modernisation programmes of
Zhou and Deng, at changes in
China's foreign policy.

# POLITICS IN THE UNITED STATES

## FROM CARTER TO REAGAN

Examines the changing political scene in the USA during the
Carter and Reagan eras and the different programmes
adopted. Charts the resurgence of congressional power and
the growth of political individualism; the operation of
presidential government; contests for national leadership; the
Republican/Conservative revival; the changing character of the
Supreme Court; the rise of ethnic politics; changes in America's
foreign policy. There is an analysis of the 1986/7 Iran-
Contragate scandal and a look at the 1988 presidential
candidates.

# CHAMBERS
# WORLD
# GAZETTEER

Editor Dr. David Munro

The international directory of facts,
figures, people and places. Over 800 pages
packed with information; 20,000 towns and
cities featured; profiles of every nation in
the world; 150 maps of key political and
administrative divisions; a 120 page atlas in
full colour.